HERE I AM,
SEEK ME

'Andy is a man possessed with the living spirit of prophetic fiery imagination. He can literally see the world made new. What I love most about Andy is in the pages of this book – he is not content only to think great thoughts or have wonderful redemptive theology, or even rest on the successes he has already seen. Andy has a fresh vision for *today* and it's full of *fire*. This man has invested his entire life in the redemption of the world and is about to increase the pace! For those of us who are amazed just watching him, he remains a living inspiration and invitation to get on with the work Jesus started. God's kingdom come!'
Danielle Strickland – speaker, advocate and author

'I vividly remember Andy's role in Festival:Manchester in 2003. Andy and I worked closely to cast the vision for the festival, unite the church around evangelism, and proclaim the gospel boldly. At the launch of the festival – after a rich time of worship and prayer – I remember Andy saying to the crowd, 'Did you feel Manchester tremble?'

'I was stirred by the comment, and it has stuck with me all these years. It seemed to clearly express Andy's vision, passion and enthusiasm, as well as his deep sensitivity to the things of God.

'From the moment I first met him, I knew the hand of God was on his life. His exuberance for spreading the Good News of Jesus and his love for people was deeply touching. Through his leadership and God's guidance,

HERE I AM, SEEK ME

More teaching from the book of Isaiah and powerful stories from The Message Trust

ANDY HAWTHORNE

WITH A FOREWORD BY **CARL BEECH**

Published by The Message Trust

Publisher:
The Message Trust
Lancaster House
Harper Road, Sharston
Manchester M22 4RG
UK

www.message.org.uk

Print Edition ISBN: 978-0-9571414-8-3

Editor: Alistair Metcalfe

Proof Reading: Dev Lunsford

Design: Message Creative
Photography: Hannah Prittie

Acknowledgements

Once again, thanks to all the devoted team at The Message Trust. What an adventure we are having!

Special thanks to Al Metcalfe, Simon Baker and the Message Creative team for helping to pull this off.

Finally, to my amazing Mum, Christine, who has prayed for me and cheered me on longer than anyone else. This book is dedicated to you because – it's fair to say – none of this would have been written without you.

Contents

FOREWORD: THE FIGHT OF MY LIFE

FOREWORD

Carl started as our UK Director in January 2016 with the brief to see life-changing Message ministries rolled out right across the nation.

I remember when I first came to Christ in 1990, soaking up the culture and vibe of what was to me, a brand new world called 'God's Kingdom'. I can distinctly remember driving home the night I met Jesus feeling like I had stepped out of a black and white picture into a full-colour, HD world and it hit me in a big way. I'll never forget driving home through Romford in Essex and realising that all the people I was passing were God's kids – but they didn't know it yet. I think for me that was the first stirring of the call of God on my life to evangelism. In fact, having been presented with a new Bible, I wrote in the front of it that I would commit the rest of my life to telling people about Jesus.

Fast forward to 1996, and at 26 years of age I was pioneering from scratch a new church on a tough estate in Essex. Having left my career in financial sales behind, I was all in for mission with my wife Karen. Working on that estate broke my heart for the poor and we did all we could to make an impact on some extremely broken lives. We pioneered food distribution, a furniture store for those placed into emergence accommodation and even a bus project that we used to place on the estate every Monday night. Little did I know that in Manchester a similar story was unfolding but in a much bigger way.

Then one day I saw the World Wide Message Tribe on a video and a full-on evangelist blasting the gospel out with such passion and focus that we all got fired up. A few years on and I was senior pastor of a large multi-congregation church and we were sending young people to join a project called Eden in Manchester. Fast forward a few more years and I was leading a national evangelistic ministry called Christian Vision for Men and taking it through a time of change and focus. Having bumped into Andy Hawthorne at a festival or two, I dropped in on him for advice and came away with an invitation to speak at one of the Message's Prayer Days.

I have to be honest that when the day came to speak to the staff in what is now an upstairs room where our Academy meets, I was a bit in awe. I mean, these guys were the people that we had all looked at in complete awe and admiration – and now I was speaking to them. I can remember to this day the word that I brought to them from Isaiah 58 and God's radical heart for the poorest of the poor, the orphan, the widow, the hungry and marginalised:

'Then your light will rise in the darkness, and your night will become like the noonday. The Lord will guide you always; he will satisfy your needs in a sun-scorched land and will strengthen your frame…. You will be like a spring whose waters never fail. Your people will rebuild the ancient ruins and will raise up age-old foundations; you will be called Repairer of Broken Walls, Restorer of Streets with Dwellings' (Isaiah 58:10-12).

These verses struck me afresh that day and my memories went right back to sitting on the London Underground and passing through desolate parts of the East End (long since regenerated) thinking that I wanted to do something about it one day. I must have been about five years old and since I was not raised as a follower of Jesus, I can only think that this was the beginning of God's call on my life to reach the hardest and toughest to reach.

And so, to cut a very long story short, Andy and I started to cheer each other on for a number of years until a moment came when I knew I had to join this crazy, full-on movement we call The Message. It felt like the completion of many years of preparation to enter into what I consider to be the fight of my life. I consider it a tremendous privilege and honour to now be leading the charge to replicate what we have established in Manchester across the UK in the poorest cities. I can honestly say that the first time I walked around the Message Enterprise Centre I felt it was a glimpse of heaven on earth – all these people who society had effectively written off being given employment, training, housing and genuine sense of family of belonging. We *desperately* need to see this rolled out across the UK along with more Edens, more creative mission, more schools work and more of whatever else the Lord reveals to us!

Our plans are bold, crazily ambitious and far bigger than we can deliver in our own strength. However, we believe that God has mandated us to 'plan big' and not allow us to just keep a vision in our heads. Doing that will keep it a dream that affects no one – and we believe God has called us to reach millions. So, as I often say, 'nothing ever happened to someone who didn't have a go.' We're going for it in a big way and we need all the prayer, cash, people and support that we can muster to see this beautiful mission delivered.

As I write this, we have just taken on new offices for a new Hub in the centre of Birmingham. Our new team for London has started to break ground. A brand-new Eden bus for Scotland is doing the business and new Eden teams stand ready to begin at a rate of one a month across the UK. The work in Wales is bringing light into tough parts of South Wales with incredible creative zeal and the Higher tour is poised to start in three cities over the next few years. Conversations have begun with serious intent to develop the full package of Message ministries into Yorkshire and the North East, and we have just started two new bands to reach out into the UK. We have four businesses in Manchester to employ people who have recently left prison, houses are being purchased and we have new residents moving into a multi-occupancy home called The Oaks. I could go on, and If you feel a bit breathless just reading that, then join the club! But we feel we have only just begun. There is so much to do! For example, did you know that about one quarter of all children in the UK live under the poverty line and that there are millions of young people in the UK who have absolutely no clue who Jesus is? This is our time and its happening on our watch, something that certainly gets me up in the morning and drives me forward to do more, try more, pray harder and use all that God has placed in my hands to make an impact.

Let me take this opportunity to reaffirm that absolutely front and centre for The Message as we build and grow across the UK is the proclamation of the message of Jesus. We believe that whilst we obviously need administrative and governmental action to reach the poor, in reality it's only the gospel of Jesus Christ that can truly transform cities and change lives. This will be a major focus of my work going forward and its part of the fabric and DNA of our movement. If you cut us in half, we bleed the gospel and whether you work in accounts, catering, IT or facilities here, you are as much on mission at The Message as if you were a front-line evangelist. There's zero compromise on that one. Take a short walk around Message HQ in Manchester and you will bump into more than a handful of people who will be keen to share that with you. It's what makes us what we are.

And so we plough on – dreaming dreams and turning them into reality as God so graces us. In the background we are looking to develop our leaders and invest heavily into raising up the next generation of missional leaders. We want to see our Academy grow and develop; around 50% of all our Academy graduates go on to work with us so it's a critical part of our work. We want to develop our skills training for those coming out of prison and I fully expect that we will see the development of fully accredited training courses from NVQ level right through to Master's degrees, with our teams members securing employment in many different spheres and trades.

A non-negotiable for all of us is Eden – and working with Sam Ward, our amazing Eden National Director, I expect that we will see exponential growth and significant impact. It's poised to be one of the fastest-growing missional movements in the UK. Every team member is an urban hero choosing to go 'downwardly mobile', to move into a poor urban estate and demonstrate the light and love of Christ. We will see more bands and creative teams fusing cutting-edge and relevant creativity whilst proclaiming ancient and timeless gospel truth. I think there will also be surprises. A movement that ducks and dives like we do is bound to stumble into new ideas that don't even exist in the far reaches of my imagination as I write this chapter. And that's what I love about being in this movement – we are open to whatever the Lord brings to us and we act on it quickly once we know it's right. We haven't got time to waste and we are all gripped by a sense of urgency to reach as many people as we can with the gospel in the short time that God has given us.

Romans 12 from verse 9 onwards contains an extraordinary mandate for kingdom living that I read over and over again. But it's topped by verse one of that chapter that calls us 'living sacrifices.' I constantly ask myself what that means for us as a movement as well as what it means for me personally. I think I can sum it up in this bold prayer that I would urge you all to pray.

'Jesus, I will follow you wherever you tell me to go, and I will do whatever you ask me to do – no matter what.'

Those that pray that prayer are taking the lid and constraints off their walk with Jesus Christ. They will be prepared to move house, trust God with their kids, give their all for the purposes of God, open their lives and homes and work with a ceaseless passion to reach the lost, the poor and the broken.

To pray that prayer is at the heart of what it means to be 'all-in' at The Message Trust. Perhaps some of you reading this resonate with that prayer and the hunger and desire to live for a cause that is greater than your own life. I truly hope so. One day we will all die – and we will be with Jesus. On that day I want to meet a whole bunch of people who are with us in eternity because we were relentless, didn't quit and went the extra mile. Here's to the next 25 years and the many, many chapters yet to be written.

— Carl Beech, Manchester, 2016

INTRODUCTION

Introduction

At The Message we make no apology for the amount of work time we spend in worship and prayer.

It's not just our monthly Prayer Days – every day starts with at least half an hour set aside to sing and pray. It's part, I believe, of what makes The Message what it is. On Tuesdays, we gather the whole team for worship and prayer and one of the Message leadership team usually shares from the Bible. Over the last three-and-a-half years, whenever I've spoken on a Tuesday morning, I've been chugging my way through the amazing book of Isaiah. And it's stunning to look back over what God has done in and through us in that time.

Among other things, we've launched 12 new Eden teams; put together two new bands; stepped up our prisons work and launched the Message Enterprise Centre to provide work, homes and supportive community to some of our region's most troubled young men and women who have come to Christ. We've stepped out with new Message ministries in the Midlands, Wales and Scotland. We've launched the Higher Tour, the most ambitious youth mission in the UK for a generation. And we've opened our first international hub in South Africa which is now delivering the full transformational 'Message package' in prisons, schools and tough communities around Cape Town. You can read more about all these things in the following pages.

About a couple of years into our Isaiah journey, I got a phone call from my friend John Bunjo who, as well as pastoring his own church in Uganda, oversees a major prayer movement and network of churches bringing transformation amongst the poorest of the poor. He is also a guy who, I know from my own experience, really hears the Lord. The phone call was to let me know that he was coming to the UK – he had been fasting and praying and really believed that he had a word from the Lord for us. So, full of expectancy, a few days later I gathered the team and John let loose on us.

His words stopped me in my tracks. In short, he said that everything was about to go to the next level for The Message. He prophesied that we were about to enter a tremendous 'season of open doors' (and over the next few weeks, I received exactly the same word from other people I respect four more times). He also said that Isaiah 60 would be very important – saying, 'Get ready to arise and shine, for the glory of the Lord is upon you!' Finally, he said, 'You, Andy, need to get away and seek the Lord over all of this'.

I have to confess that my heart sank a little on hearing this, knowing that John was probably thinking about a full 21 days of fasting and prayer in the desert, and that when I looked at my diary I would probably struggle to find a spare day in the following few weeks. But with some juggling, I managed to find a couple of days and set off for a short retreat in the Lake District.

On the way up the motorway I listened to a talk called 'Keeping Your Vision Hot' in the car, from my friend Paul Hallam, the irrepressible leader of Lighthouse Church in Manchester. I was so encouraged that his whole talk was based on – guess what? – Isaiah 60 and so much of it seemed immensely relevant to where we were at with The Message.

During the day I walked in the hills, talking to the Lord, then came back to my hotel room and knelt down by my bed to read the Bible. I was planning to read from the book of Romans as this was where I had been studying, but as I placed my Bible on the bed it fell open to – guess where? – Isaiah 60! In the following few hours I had what can only be described as an extraordinary time with the Lord in his Word. It was as if the past 26 years of The Message was unfolding before me...

'Arise, shine, for your light has come....' as John Bunjo had already said.

'The righteousness of your cause will shine like the noonday sun...'
– One of our touchstone scriptures since the beginning of The Message.

'The least will become a thousand, the smallest a mighty nation...'
– Our heartbeat as a movement from the very beginning.

'They are the shoot I have planted, the work of my hands for the display of my splendour...' – again, right at the start of The Message, God spoke to me through Isaiah 43 in particular promising that the wild animals (a good description for some of the young people we were working with) would come to honour him.

'Those I formed for myself that they may proclaim my praise....'
– it was all brilliantly encouraging stuff.

As I prayed these words back to the Lord, I was particularly drawn to Isaiah 60 verse 4 – 'Lift your eyes and look about you, all assemble...'

I felt like the Lord was saying it was time to 'go big again' – in other words, to book some big venues, put the lamp on a stand and preach the gospel loud and clear. Of course, it's not like that's anything new for us. The Message has always been well known for bold, 'big stage' evangelism, right back to the days of The World Wide Message Tribe and even before that. But I wonder if it's fair to say that for the last few years we'd been concentrating our attention mostly on grassroots work, reaching the hardest to reach young people with Eden and our incarnational work with prisoners and ex-offenders.

I clearly felt God saying it was time to shift the balance back, and it was on the back of this that the vision for the Higher Tour was developed. We plan to travel the length and breadth of the country, praying hard and preaching the good news, believing for a culture-changing number of new disciples – you can read all about it in Chapter 7. The other thing I sensed the Lord saying during this time away was that as much as I would love to, I wasn't to be the main preacher at any of these large events. The best thing I could do was to train and mentor a bunch of multiplying, younger evangelists – hence the Advance evangelist network (see more, starting on page 54).

This is the second book I've written on Isaiah. The first one which also included many 'only God' testimonies was called *Here I Am, Send Me*. As I prepared the material for this book, it hit me afresh that the only hope we have of serving the Lord and saying 'here I am, send me' is because he took the initiative in the first place and invited us to change the world for good on his behalf. Hence the title of this new book, *Here I Am, Seek Me*.

I love Isaiah 58, particularly as the Lord promises that if we will get off our own agenda and be concerned with the things that are on his heart – the least, last and lost – then 'our light really will break forth' and our 'healing will quickly come' (v.8). The Lord himself will say 'Here I am' when that happens in and through ordinary people like us, and the world won't know what hit it.

In the time it took me to teach through Isaiah week-by-week, so much happened in the life of The Message. God has been so good. We began working in Scotland, Wales and the Midlands – and South Africa! We got four new Eden buses on the road. We launched Edens in Latchford, Parkhead, Partington, Shoreditch, Southwick, Tremorfa, Walsall, Weoley Castle and Wyrley Birch – not to mention Salt River, Pelican Park and Nyanga in South Africa. We trained and commissioned two new bands, BrightLine and Vital Signs, both of whom have already won loads of souls for Jesus. Four years ago we hadn't even thought about The Message Enterprise Centre. And we certainly hadn't dreamt we'd be doing The Higher Tour.

I hope this book encourages you to seek the Lord for the things that are on his heart, and to expect greater things as you go in his name.

WAKE-UP
CALL

CHAPTER ONE

ISAIAH 17:1, 6-7

A prophecy against Damascus:

'See, Damascus will no longer be a city

but will become a heap of ruins…

Yet some gleanings will remain,

as when an olive tree is beaten,

leaving two or three olives on the topmost branches,

four or five on the fruitful boughs,'

declares the Lord,

the God of Israel.

In that day people will look to their Maker

and turn their eyes to the Holy One of Israel.

Isaiah 17:1, 6-7

"

Isaiah 17 is a healthy reminder that we need to wake up a bit when we read our Bibles

The best advice I've ever heard on reading the Bible is 'just keep going' – especially through the bits that feel like hard work. I remember when I first became a Christian, the evangelist Eric Delve told me, 'Some of the Bible is like chocolate and champagne, other bits are like cabbage. But we need both.' Eric is absolutely right: we need a balanced diet of some of the harder bits of the Old Testament alongside the easier-to-understand, more exciting bits of the New Testament. Parts of Isaiah are this way, too – a bit obscure, a bit hard work. But sometimes, the prophecies inside this extraordinary book seem to collide directly with our present-day world, and make us seriously stop and think.

Recently my wife Michele and I met up with two missionary friends, wonderful people who were working in the Arab world and have come back to Manchester to plant a church among the Muslim community in the city. They've set up a stall on a local market, giving away, and selling very cheaply, Bibles in Farsi and Arabic and other Christian books. They told us that the day before, they'd baptised five people, and four of them were Iranians. They commented that it feels a bit like cheating because it's so easy to lead Iranians to Jesus at the moment: 'It's like shelling peas. You talk to any Farsi speaker and they are just so soft to the gospel. They're jumping into the kingdom.' You might think that Iranians would be among the hardest to reach with their brutal, strict Islamic regime, but our friends told us that the system there is falling apart. they said. 'What we are seeing happening with the Arab Spring, what we've seen in Egypt and Syria, it's horrible, but it's leading to an amazing opportunity for the gospel of Jesus.'

But it was what they said next that really got me thinking: 'All of these events that are happening in the Middle East – we're living in the very last days of Planet Earth before it all comes together.' What a thought! Now, I don't know whether they're right or not. Maybe we need to go back to our Bibles again, look at the newspapers at what's happening and think hard: could it be the case? Could we be living in the most exciting generation in world history, just before Jesus returns?

Look and be amazed

One thing's for sure: lots and lots of things are going to happen in the Middle East because that's where all the prophecies in the Bible are focused. They are the Bible lands – Israel and its surrounding countries. So much of what's going on in the world when you switch on the news is in those very territories: the places where the Bible was written, the places where Jesus walked, the nations all the prophecies are about. Today the Lord says, 'Look, and be amazed at what is happening around these countries in the Middle East'.

Isaiah 17 is a healthy reminder that we need to wake up a bit when we read our Bibles. It contains an oracle against Damascus – a place we regularly hear mentioned on the nightly news because of the horrific stuff going on there. The sort of stuff that's prophesied in the book of Isaiah is happening before our eyes.

Remember that Isaiah is always prophesying to three horizons. His message is that something is going to happen *soon* in Syria, Egypt, Moab, Philistia and the surrounding countries – in other words, things are going to happen north, south, east, west of Israel. Then something is going to happen in this territory *in a few hundred years' time* when the Messiah comes that's going to accelerate all of this. And then finally something is going to happen *at the end of time*, also in this region. These areas on the news every night, these are the exact territories that Isaiah prophesied into.

The people of God should clearly have one eye on the Word and one eye on the world, reading our newspapers saying, 'Lord, help us to understand what's going on.' I pray that God will build an expectancy in our hearts. If we do this, maybe a greater expectancy will come in our hearts.

What a good thing it would be for the people of God if we thought 'Wow, Jesus may just return very soon'. I think it would track everything. It would affect the way we play games with sin. Maybe it would affect the way we spend our money. Maybe it would even affect our evangelism – if we thought that we'd soon be with Jesus for all eternity, and we'd had a part to play in getting other people there. It's a bit of a wake-up call for us, isn't it?

Live differently

Read the next few chapters of Isaiah and see this theme opening out. We've already had prophecies about Moab which was to the east, prophecies against Philistia which is to the west; soon we'll have prophecies to the south which is Egypt, and here we have prophecies to the north which is Syria. Each prophecy carries the same tension – of judgment leading to salvation; of fire burning stuff up but it's all part of God's purposes. It's God working out his purposes through fearful judgment, ultimately to see his salvation plan.

Repentance which leads to blessing is what the Lord is looking for, both then and now. God was constantly saying to his people 'Whatever you do, do not live like those around you; do not live like those to the north, east, south and west who are worshipping things made by their own hands, who are given over to sin, who are just going down a road of destruction. Do not live like them, live differently, repent.' It's the same today, 3000 years later. We need to learn that our personal repentance is central to our wider purpose. If we want to live the big vision God has for us, if we want to see the multiplication God has promised, we have to be walking in repentance.

At The Message if we want to see the gospel proclaimed, communities transformed, prisoners set free, both here and around the world, we need to be hating sin. We need to be looking at the nations around us, looking at the lost and saying, 'we're not going to live like that, we're going to stand out as different.'

Satan is very subtle and seductive, and he has always got another step down for you. He's always got a nasty, dirty image on your computer screen, he's always got another door you can open into addiction. We've got to be a people who say, 'No, I'm going to be quick to repent of that stuff, I'm not going to go there… why would I want to go there when I've got a bigger, wider purpose? I'm part of the chosen people of God. I'm chosen to make a mark in this generation.'

A day is coming

It can sometimes feel like there's not many of us who are committed to this path, and Isaiah speaks to this too. In Isaiah's time Israel's glory has been wasting away – and there aren't many olives left on the tree (see verse 6). I think we've been through a little season like that in our nation. In 1955, over 50% of people went to church, and roughly the same percentage were people in their 20s. By 2005, that had gone down to well under 10% of the whole population and just 3% of people were in their 20s.

It feels like we've had 50 years of pruning. This nation – a fruitful olive grove that was at the centre of world mission for so long, which translated the scriptures and sent out the gospel into the far ends of the Earth – today has just a few olives left on the top of a bare tree. But life has started to spring out again. There's ample evidence that God's not finished with us yet. Things are turning around – we're seeing it in our work at The Message and churches are seeing it all over the country, too.

This picture that was for Israel is for us too: men will again 'look to their Maker' (verse 7), they'll turn away from their 'Asherah poles and the things that their fingers have made' (8), they'll turn away from all this man-made stuff and they'll turn back to God. Sounds good, doesn't it?

Our nation has bought into all this rubbish and it's only led to crime, misery, divorce, suicide and abuse. But all that's going to turn around as we turn back to God and the spring starts to come up on the olive grove because 'some gleanings remain' as Isaiah put it (6). I love the fact that there's such a of sense of destiny about Isaiah 17 and that phrase keeps coming back – 'in that day... in that day'. You know there is a day coming for the tide to turn, a day for repentance to lead to salvation, judgment to be followed by glory, and I want to live in that day. But it's only going to happen when God's people get their act together.

It's yet another reminder from Isaiah that we're not playing games here. It's serious how we live, it's serious how we pray, it's serious how we fight sin. There's so much at stake. So how about it? How about repenting of anything that competes in our hearts for the number one slot? How about turning our backs on any little sin and placing Jesus there at number one, putting his gospel where it belongs?

As I was writing this, an email popped up from a forum I've been invited to be a part of. One phrase stood out for me: 'The gospel of Christ is not just private, personal opinion, the gospel is public truth'. That's it in a nutshell: it's not just about me and my own private walk with Jesus, it's about a whole nation that must know that Jesus is Lord. We will give him all the glory, we will give him all the praise and we will fully expect that the praise spills out.

Somebody has got to love this gospel so much that they want to put it on a stand, that they're prepared to fight sin, they're prepared to pray like they've never prayed before, to do stuff we've never done before to reach more people than we've ever reached before. Let's be those people.

REFLECTION

1. Which parts of Bible study do you struggle with the most? Who could you ask for help to go deeper into God's Word?

2. Do you make a regular habit of meditating on the Word in the light of the daily news and bring the needs of the world before the Lord?

3. Praise God for signs that the tide is turning in our nation back towards holiness in the church and fruitfulness in our mission.

PRAYER

This nation needs to know you, Lord Jesus.

Make my life a song of praise that spills out. See my desire today to give you more of me and reach more people for you than ever before.

Amen

'I was dealing death –
now I'm dealing life. It's
only God who does that.'

Andy adds: Mo's story is an amazing testimony of the power of God who both saves and sends. He had a dramatic encounter with God just before he went to prison for dealing drugs and Mo began to believe that God was sending him into the prisons for a purpose. During that time he saw more than 600 men giving their lives to Christ. Today he continues to see many lives transformed through his story and he has planted a thriving new church in Hull. He is also a member of my Advance group and himself mentors lots of young evangelists.

I was raised on a tough estate in Peckham, South London. It was a place where tensions towards the police were always simmering, and sometimes bubbled over. Unlike many young men on the estate, I knew my father – and even respected him growing up. But as I entered my teenage years, he walked out on me and my mum.

I looked up to him and at the same time I despised him. He was a professional, a lawyer, and he always encouraged me to study hard, to do my homework. But he left. He wasn't physically there. Our relationship was always long distance, over the phone, seeing me at weekends.

When I was 12 I started hanging out with a group of men on the estate who seemed to have everything I understood as success. They had respect, the best clothes, BMWs, nice watches and chains. My dad was ringing me to check in once a week – but these guys were there in front of me every day.

By the age of 14, I was selling cannabis in order to feed my own growing addiction. At just 15, I was stabbed five times after an altercation with a local gang – one wound missing my spine by inches. By 18, I was making £8,000 a month dealing crack cocaine and heroin on the south coast.

But just a year later I was busted by undercover police.

Shortly before I was picked up, I'd met a girl, who would later become my wife. She'd told me all about how she was a Christian and that she had a personal relationship with Jesus. This was all meaningless to me – I was raised in the Muslim faith.

So I finally swallowed my pride and prayed: "Jesus, if you're really there, help me get out of this situation." Within two or three minutes, there was a knock on the cell door and an officer appeared. He said, "You were supposed to go to prison tomorrow. But you're being let out until we're ready for you."

Honestly, I was hungry for God. I had never read the Bible up to that point – now I couldn't get enough of it. I was at every church service, helping out wherever I could. I even started preaching.

I then started to accept that if it was God's will for me to go to prison, then I would serve him there.

I ending up serving 18 months of a three-year sentence, but from the moment I landed, I knew what I was there for. I wasn't in prison as a gangster and a drug dealer. I was in prison as a gospel-preaching

(Clockwise from top left): street evangelism; with wife, Elizabeth;
PH Hull church; preaching at Higher Manchester 2016

Christian! I've got an audience – and my audience can't go anywhere!

Then people started coming to me with their problems and officers would ask me to speak to certain men about issues they were facing. It was a massive mission field.

I saw the Sunday chapel service grow from five men to over 100 as rapists, murderers, thieves were getting saved. Over the next 18 months I moved prisons three times. During that time I had the privilege of seeing around 600 young men commit their lives to Christ, as I simply shared my personal testimony and preached.

When I was at the final prison HMYOI Thorn Cross, I met members of the Message in Prisons team. What started happening was that towards the end of my sentence, my faith was drying out, to be honest. I'd been giving out non-stop for months, with almost nothing coming in. It was such a blessing to have someone reaching out to me, and helping me build some roots of my own.

After I got out of prison in 2009, The Message really kicked into my life. It was a big deal adapting back to life on the outside. I married my girlfriend Elizabeth four weeks after I got out. You can imagine, after being locked up with a bunch of guys for 18 months, I wasn't the best husband. I also had no job, I couldn't find one. I felt like a shadow of myself.

During this time, my church was a great support and many of the Message guys took the time to invest in me.

The first two guys I led to Christ in prison were from Hull and during the next six years I had that city on my heart. Then in May 2015 myself and my wife planted a church in one of the roughest parts of Hull. We've already grown from just the two of us to more than 130 people. We've seen many young people getting saved with 30 commitments on one Sunday alone.

I'm still involved with The Message Trust. It was fantastic preaching and sharing my testimony at their recent Higher tour when hundreds of young people got saved.

I'm also part of a group called Advance led by Andy Hawthorne gathering regularly with several other evangelists to sharpen our skills in sharing the Gospel.

I do preach around the country as well but I've turned down some events because I'm pastoring my church. I try not to be away too much, but the good thing is when I do leave it gives the young evangelists I mentor the opportunity to put their skills into practice and we've seen some as young as 16 preaching in our church.

As a dealer I handed out something that killed people. A few years later I'm handing out something that gives them life. I was dealing death – now I'm dealing life. It's only God who does that.

WELCOME TO THE BANQUET

CHAPTER TWO

ISAIAH 25:6-9

On this mountain the Lord Almighty will prepare

a feast of rich food for all peoples,

a banquet of aged wine –

the best of meats and the finest of wines.

On this mountain he will destroy

the shroud that enfolds all peoples,

the sheet that covers all nations;

he will swallow up death for ever.

The Sovereign Lord will wipe away the tears

from all faces;

he will remove his people's disgrace

from all the earth.

The Lord has spoken.

In that day they will say,

'Surely this is our God;

we trusted in him, and he saved us.

This is the Lord, we trusted in him;

let us rejoice and be glad in his salvation.'

Isaiah 25:6-9

If we do believe that death will be swallowed up in victory forever, isn't it time we started living like it?

We all know names are really important ('Andy' means 'manly' – I'm quite proud of that!) Names can be spoken over us for good and for bad. But all of us have the name of Isaiah spoken over us – because Isaiah means 'the Lord saves'. Where would we be if it wasn't for Jesus? We'd be lost, but we've been saved. As we look at some of the difficult verses in Isaiah it's important we keep at the front of our minds that yes, there are fearful things in the scriptures about judgment and chaos if we ignore God's voice, but that is not the final word. The Lord's final word over any life (or any nation) is always salvation.

When we're saved, when we get given the name Isaiah, we're saved for all eternity. There's a future that's bright and we get a little glimpse of it in Isaiah 25. But we also get a down-payment, a deposit on that salvation. We get the little taste of it – about 0.0000000001% of what the Lord's got for us in eternity – and yes, it is breathtaking. We get saved from wasting our lives and living the broken, messed-up life that the devil had planned for us before the Lord set us free.

Isaiah 25 gives us a picture of heaven – and it's a picture of a banquet. There is a day when you're going to taste what the Lord has been preparing just for you for all eternity. The sacrifices you had to make this side of heaven will all be forgotten when you taste that 'aged wine' that the Lord's prepared and the 'finest meat' – it'll be one amazing party.

Enjoy it all

What's the first command the Lord gives in Genesis 2? Well, we all know that the first command is not to eat of the fruit of the tree of the knowledge of good and evil because you'll die, right? Actually, no! That's not the first command the Lord gives. The first command the Lord gives is Genesis 2:16, '... and the Lord God commanded the man; you are free to eat from any tree in the garden'.

In the original language it means 'eat, eat' – go on, enjoy the fruit from every tree in the garden. I've prepared some amazing trees, this is the eternal garden, this is the best of the best that I've prepared. You are free to run, skip round naked, eating from every tree in the garden, just loving life and enjoying what I've made. What a picture: eat, eat, go and enjoy it all, every last bit… apart from one tree. There's just one tree I don't want you to go near, because if you eat of that tree you'll die.

So why would you disobey God? Why would you sleep around, take drugs, get drunk, be jealous or proud? Why would you go against God's will for your life, why would you want to choose death over life? Why would you want to do that when the Lord's got all this for you and says 'eat, eat, enjoy life'? That's the story of Isaiah isn't it – why would you want to make a choice like that, you dummy, when you can live life to the full? You can enjoy good relationships, good marriages, and success in every area of your life *if you'll just do what God says.*

God's word over us is salvation and Isaiah brings the clearest teaching in the Old Testament on resurrection when he says, 'he will swallow up death forever, the sovereign Lord will wipe away the tears' (verse 8). It sounds like the New Testament, doesn't it? It sounds like the gospel. It sounds like 'Where, oh death, is your sting' (1 Corinthians 15:55)… 'The Sovereign Lord will wipe away the tears from all faces, he will remove his people's disgrace from all the earth. The Lord has spoken'.

This message of salvation is for all people and all the Earth. It's for Saudi Arabia; it's for the United Arab Emirates. It's for North Korea; it's for the hardest, worst, most anti-Christian places on earth. It's for Muslim strongholds, it's for Hindus. All people need to hear about this salvation, they need to hear about the incredible gospel of love and joy, about the banquet that God's prepared for them. They need to hear about eternity.

One thing counts

So many people this world idolises are putting their hope in the wrong basket. Steve Jobs gave an inspirational address to college graduates just before he died – it's a brilliant speech, except it's all based *here*. This incredible man, incredible businessman, incredible communicator, genius mind… but his whole life was based *here*. He said, 'I think every day, "What would I do if I died tomorrow?" and I make sure that I've done everything I need to do in this life.' How tragic to be the most brilliant businessman on Earth but end up placing everything in one basket – and finding out when you die it's the wrong basket.

I really like Beyoncé. She's a beautiful woman and sometimes her message is good, especially when she says: 'Hey girls, you don't need to have cosmetic surgery to look beautiful; you don't need to doll yourself up, you can just be beautiful.' Her whole thing is all about having a beautiful voice, a beautiful marriage, beautiful relationships. But it's all in the wrong basket, isn't it? One day, Beyoncé is going to stand before the Lord and no amount of multimillion record sales, no amount of beautiful singing, no amount of amazing achievements on this earth will mean diddly squat, will it?

What about the richest man on Earth, Bill Gates, a man who has committed to giving away everything before he dies? What a thing! What a provocation to other multi-billionaires, surely the thing Jesus would want him to do, giving his life to counteract disease and bless the poor. But even that's not going to be enough to save you is it? Even giving all your 60 billion to the poor is not going to be enough to save you.

Our final destination

I think we need to settle this in our hearts. If we do believe that death will be swallowed up in victory forever, isn't it time we started living like it? Isn't it time to do all we can to experience the banquet and invite as many people as possible on this Earth? Shouldn't we live like there will be a resurrection day for us all because we know Jesus?

One of the stories I have often told over the years is about when my dad died. He had heart disease and they sent him back from the hospital because eventually there was nothing more they could do for him. There he was, fading out of this life and into the next. On his very last night on earth, he was fighting for breath, on death's door and he said 'Christine, sing for me.' My Mum pulled out Mission Praise and she started singing all the songs she knew, starting with A, 'Abba Father let me be.' Probably about eight hours later – she got to 'Turn your eyes upon Jesus' – my Dad took his last breath. The Lord's presence was heavy in that room and my Mum got a picture, a vision, of my Dad being carried by Jesus into a beautiful garden. Ken, his brother, was there: 'Hey George, wait till you see what the Lord's got prepared for you. George, it's amazing here, you won't want to go back, it's amazing!' He walked into this garden and some of his old Christian friends who died ahead of him were there waiting. What a picture! He walked through that garden and there was a table with aged wine and the best meat and the Lord was there. The presence of the Lord was there – what a comfort, what a comfort to know that. That's what we live for, that's what it's all about and that's forever!

Songs of praise

I love the fact that Isaiah 25 is topped and tailed with songs of praise. There's this incredible picture of heaven and eternity and all that the Lord's prepared for us and it's topped with a hymn: *'Lord you are my God, I will exalt you and praise your name'* (1). If you've got heaven, if you know where you're going, if you truly believe that you're going there for all eternity then you'll develop a personal walk with Jesus.

I had a young person who's been a Christian for about ten years say to me recently, 'I didn't really know I had to pray and read the Bible every day'. She'd had no idea. How could that happen? But she told me how much a difference it had made since she'd started doing it. As you pray and read the Bible every day, as you work on your walk with Jesus, suddenly heaven will become more and more attractive and more and more you will bring heaven to earth.

But this passage ends not with a personal hymn of praise, but a corporate one: 'Surely this is our God, we trusted in him and he saved us' (9). We need both – personal songs of praise, and corporate ones, and unless you're developing both, you aren't going to get that full picture of heaven. You're never going to become the man or woman of God he wants you to be unless you work on those spiritual disciplines personally – discipline in prayer, discipline in your study of the word, discipline in mission (because yes, mission's a discipline too).

At the same time, we need to work on the corporate expression of that discipleship because we're called to be community, a family. That can be messy sometimes – we can get upset and hurt one another – but we're family. We're going to be quick to forgive and we're going to think the best of each other and spur each other on.

REFLECTION

1. Spend some time imagining the kind of banquet God has prepared for you. Who will you most delight in seeing again? What will work, rest and play look like in heaven for you?

2. How's your personal walk with God going? What does your personal song of praise to Jesus sound like – loud and boisterous, or gentle and intimate? Which do you need to work on?

3. What aspects of corporate discipleship – i.e. church, fellowship group or outreach – do you struggle with? What might God be trying to teach you through that?

PRAYER

Beautiful Lord Jesus, grow in my heart a hunger for heaven. Give me just enough tastes of the banquet to come to keep me restless to share your invitation with others. Help me to learn a deeper discipline of prayer, study and mission so that I make this short life count for eternity.

Amen

'It's often step by step
whether it's a small or
big breakthrough'

Andy adds: Tash was one of the young people reached by Eden Hattersley, one of our early Eden teams, and one with an amazing legacy. She's an example of how our Eden workers never give up on young people – even when their challenging behaviour makes them almost impossible to work with. The fact that she's now giving her own life to helping other vulnerable people shows just how powerful this ministry is.

Before the Eden team came to Hattersley my family life was quite chaotic. There was quite a lot of physical and emotional abuse growing up. As I became a teenager, at the most crucial point of trying to figure life out, I still felt a lot of fear and anger.

I wasn't the most well behaved due to the environment I was in. So at the age of 14 when the Eden team arrived I was at a point when I was suffering depression. My parents had just split up as well. I just didn't know what I wanted to do with no plans for the future. I just thought I'd be on benefits for the rest of my life.

As a coping mechanism I was drinking and taking drugs to try and get rid of what I was feeling. I just didn't feel confident without taking something.

I remember meeting the Eden team for the first time feeling quite excited. I could see something in them that was different and was very appealing, but then on the other hand I was in a different world. My friends thought they were brainwashing me with the faith side of stuff. It wasn't until later on that I was able to grasp the Christian faith.

Before then I'd had no great experience of faith. Sometimes I'd gone to church just because we'd get a Sunday dinner afterwards. But I'd never really thought about it.

Initially I tested them with my behaviour because I found it difficult to trust anyone. I wasn't disruptive but I was quite cheeky. I desperately wanted to hear more about their Christian faith, but I didn't trust what they had to say. My mum also said she didn't want me to be any part of them. But when I was with them I felt different and wanted to know more so I kept going to their youth meetings.

Over the next five years they became a major part of my world. They didn't just invite me to church and chat to me. But they stepped in at a time when I needed major surgery. It wasn't my parents taking me to these appointments, it was the Eden team. They became family and they became people who I wanted to be like.

When I was 19, the Eden team leader, Sharon Murphy, said I should get out of the area where I lived to be free socially from my friends who were still taking drugs. It was the lifestyle that I couldn't get out of.

So I moved to Old Trafford to be part of Message Academy (at that time, called Genetik) run by the Message Trust. But even then I was scared to trust God. But the turning point came when I went on a six-month mission trip to Zimbabwe with The Message.

When I told my mum I wanted to go to Africa she said if I went there I couldn't

come home, but for the first time I felt like God was calling me to go. Being away in a different country is where I found my faith and a place where I was helping others and I was free to be who I was. No one was taking drugs or drinking alcohol. I left the airport a smoker and over there we weren't able to smoke. So a lot of my lifestyle changed and that's when I grasped God fully. I knew there was a God and I could see him in other people's lives.

But when I came back from Africa I moved back into Hattersley and the same cycle began to happen as the same temptations came back. Then Sharon told me they were opening up Eden in Sheffield and asked me if I'd become one of their youth workers so I took the opportunity to get out of Manchester.

But I realised I couldn't run away from all the hurt and pain. One evening I was sexually assaulted by two men. I remember walking the streets after leaving the property I was in and crying. I had never felt so alone.

I knew that the Eden team was always there and so I called Sharon. She came with her husband and brought me back to her house. I never spoke to her about what happened. I didn't tell anyone as I told myself it was my fault. When I was with her I knew I was safe. She arranged for the team to be with me the next day.

There were various similar situations which my lifestyle led me into, as I continued on a cycle of drinking, drugs, suicide idolisation and self-harm. I believed it was helping me to cope with the emotional pain I had been carrying from childhood.

That is what made me make the decision of going into the City Hearts Restore programme in Sheffield which helps vulnerable women deal with abuse and addictions.

During this time I was able to talk about how it had been at home and what I'd been through and I had the freedom to let everything out. After completing the programme, I found I was finally free from my past.

Over the past five years I've been trained in counselling and dealing with people with addictive behaviour and now I'm working there full-time.

I'm an assistant coordinator for the Restore programme working with women with life controlling issues such as self-harm, eating disorders, depression, drug and alcohol abuse. Also I'm a case worker for the anti-trafficking side of City Hearts.

It's indescribable, when I look back to how I was when I was in a place of wanting to end my life and having low self-worth which is now completely gone. When I sit with women I just see it as such an honour and privilege to be in the place that I am at.

I'm just so grateful that the Eden team came into my life. If they hadn't come to my estate, I'd still be where I was with no hope for a future. Now, I am helping other women step into freedom. It's often step by step whether it's a small or big breakthrough. They've been walking in fear like I did. The highlight is being part of them doing the day to day living and moving forward in their lives.

SIX THINGS ONLY JESUS CAN DO

CHAPTER THREE

"

Isaiah gives us a foretaste of Christ more than 600 years before he walked on this Earth

You've probably gathered by now that much of Isaiah involves some very severe warnings of judgment. God brings these warnings, not because he wants to *judge* people but because he wants to *save* people. Why did Jesus speak so much about hell – more than he did about heaven? Simple – because he didn't want anyone to go there! We don't see heaven clearly enough unless we've got a picture of hell. We don't see how great our salvation is until we realise how fearful judgment is.

But in the midst of all this scary talk, suddenly there's this incredible shaft of light in Isaiah 35. It's actually one of my favourite chapters in the whole Bible – because what Isaiah prophesies here is God's plan is for every person. This is what's available to everybody who God's ever made. This is what we present in schools and tough communities and prisons – this incredible salvation picture. Isaiah gives us a foretaste of Christ more than 600 years before he walked on this Earth, and in ten powerful verses shows us six things only Jesus can do.

1. Empty people become full people

The desert and the parched land will be glad;
   the wilderness will rejoice and blossom.
Like the crocus, it will burst into bloom;
   it will rejoice greatly and shout for joy.
The glory of Lebanon will be given to it,
   the splendour of Carmel and Sharon;
they will see the glory of the Lord,
   the splendour of our God. (Isaiah 35:1-2)

One of my favourite Message stories from the last few years is of Michael Ward, who was our Urban Hero of the Year in 2015. Today he's a lovely, sweet, gentle Irish brother – but ask his family about what he was like just a few years ago and it's a totally different picture. They'll tell you what a crazy guy he was, what a madman he was; how violent and dangerous he was. Michael met Jesus in prison and came out a completely different man. Before prison, Michael was an empty man, suicidal, but Jesus met him and changed his life.

Michael had been going out with his lovely wife Ciana for only a week when he was sent to prison for three and half years. But she fell in love with him and waited for him. Out of prison comes this completely different man who leads her to Christ as well as two of his cousins who have also come to Christ and have since been baptised. Michael's been a Christian 18 months and one by one he's leading everybody he knows to Jesus. All that needs to happen is for us to do what Michael is doing and the world will be saved!

Everywhere Jesus starts to move this is what happens. People whose lives can be described as deserts become rivers when he's around – don't you love him? This is our gospel; only he can do that!

2. Weak people become strong people

> Strengthen the feeble hands,
>   steady the knees that give way (Isaiah 35:3)

When you're really scared, the first places it shows is in your hands and knees – you feel your hands shaking and your knees knocking. Well, here Isaiah gives us a picture of weak people becoming strong.

Do you ever feel weak? Do you ever feel a little bit useless? Do you ever feel a little bit small? Well, good! Because here's a wonderful scripture for you: *'My grace is sufficient for you, for my power is made perfect in weakness. Therefore, I'll boast all the more gladly about my weaknesses so that Christ's power may rest on me. That is why for Christ's sake, I delight in weaknesses. In insults, in hardships, in persecutions and in difficulties for when I am weak, then I am strong'* (2 Corinthians 12:8-10). It's OK to feel weak because it's not about *what* we have going for us, it's about *who* we have inside of us – and we have the living God inside of us.

Not long ago I was asked to give an address in the Houses of Parliament. I'll never forget looking out at all the MPs, the Speaker, the business leaders assembled there. All I had was a simple talk called 'The Bible works, Jesus works.' All of a sudden a little voice in my head said, 'Andy, this is pathetic – these people are much too clever for this.' I was just about to scrub it and ask God to give me something a bit more impressive. But then I felt, 'No, stuff it! This is all I've got. I'm a simple, weak guy but I've got a message that can change lives.' When God gets hold of an ordinary person and he's in them, the weak become strong.

3. Fearful people become faith-filled people

Say to those with fearful hearts,
    'Be strong, do not fear;
your God will come,
    he will come with vengeance;
with divine retribution
    he will come to save you.' (Isaiah 35:4)

Something's got to happen when there's a group of people who have faith in Christ because God has promised to move on their behalf. Look at the language here: does it say your God *might* come? No, it says your God *will* come. He will come! So let's do all we can to remove the virus of fear that inflicts so many Christian lives and so many ministries, so many churches, which holds us back from all we're meant to become. Nothing is impossible for people who have faith.

When we've discovered the sure and certain word of God we'd better take some risks. We'd better remove that virus of fear and step out in faith because it's only faith-filled people who change the world and it only ever will be. Fearful people just curl up in the corner and do nothing. Faithful people get on with it and step out.

The only thing I think we need more fear of in the church in our nation is a bit more fear of hell. People are heading for a lost eternity and we have the answer. We need to be fearful for those who are lost.

4. Sick people will become well

Then will the eyes of the blind be opened
    and the ears of the deaf unstopped.
Then will the lame leap like a deer,
    and the mute tongue shout for joy.
Water will gush forth in the wilderness
    and streams in the desert. (Isaiah 35:5-6)

Jesus can make sick people well and we must keep on praying for the sick, day in, day out, keep believing for healing to flow. If we're seeing a trickle of healing, let's believe for a river – let's not stop praying for those who are sick. If we don't see the full measure yet, let's not give up!

Commentators say that the miracle of opening the eyes of the blind was reserved only for the Messiah. You don't find prophets opening the eyes of the blind in the Bible, only the Messiah. A great friend of The Message, Alan Morton, was telling us about a child in their church who was going blind. Every time they had a big time of prayer the sight would get slightly better – not fully better, not fully restored, but a little better every time they prayed. Sometimes we just have to knock and keep on knocking, keep believing.

Every miracle of Jesus was a double miracle: it was a healing but it was also a fulfilment of prophecy, a reminder that the Messiah had come. Every time we see a miracle, every time we see sick people becoming well there's a double blessing. Yes, there's a blessing for that person but there's a fulfilment of prophecy: Jesus is present with us to heal.

5. Thirsty people will become satisfied people

> The burning sand will become a pool,
>> the thirsty ground bubbling springs.
> In the haunts where jackals once lay,
>> grass and reeds and papyrus will grow. (Isaiah 35:7)

There's only one qualification you need to receive life-giving water from Jesus. Do you know what it is? Just be thirsty! Be thirsty for his presence, be thirsty for his power. Thirst is one of our strongest desires. I love Isaiah 55 where the Lord says, 'Come, come to the waters, come'.

It's a divine invitation, a picture of a water carrier walking into desperately dry desert places with a big leather water carrier. The water carrier would come into the village 'Ho, ho, ho anyone thirsty?' and they would come and give him a few shekels for water. The Lord in Isaiah 55 says 'Ho, anyone thirsty, come, buy, without money, without price, it's free'. The only qualification is just to be thirsty.

Thirsty people will be satisfied. Come to the waters, the Lord says, if you're thirsty, come to me! I've got plenty of life-giving water to pour into your soul, to change everything. And finally, the sixth thing only Jesus can do:

6. Sinful people become holy people

> And a highway will be there;
>> it will be called the Way of Holiness;
>> it will be for those who walk on that Way.
> The unclean will not journey on it;
>> wicked fools will not go about on it.
> No lion will be there,
>> nor any ravenous beast;
>> they will not be found there.
> But only the redeemed will walk there,
> and those the Lord has rescued will return.
> They will enter Zion with singing;
>> everlasting joy will crown their heads.
> Gladness and joy will overtake them,
> and sorrow and sighing will flee away. (Isaiah 35:8-10)

I don't know what your present is like but I'll tell you what your future will be if you know Jesus... it's this! Gladness and joy will overtake you, sorrow and sighing will flee away. It can happen because of Jesus. Thanks to him, a sinful person becomes a holy person, walking on a highway of holiness. They have the sure and certain destination of Heaven.

I deserve all the judgment of the Old Testament – I deserve the lot. I'm a hopeless sinner, I'm a sinful man, I deserve the full wrath of God on my life because I rebelled against him in thought, attitude and desire. But that is not my future because Jesus took the full measure of all that judgment, all that wrath on himself, there on the cross. How can we keep that to ourselves? Everywhere we look, sinful people can become holy people, made right and acceptable to God, on a highway of holiness and heading towards a destination where gladness and joy will overtake them, where sorrow and sighing will flee away. What a gospel!

REFLECTION

1. Read Isaiah 35 slowly again. Which of the promises gives you most hope today? Who can you share this hope with?

2. In what ways do you feel your own weakness most keenly? Are you naturally shy? Are you especially self-conscious in some way? How might God be using it to fulfil his purposes?

3. Bring before the Lord someone you know is sick in mind, body or spirit. Contend for them in prayer and commit to keep on praying for them.

PRAYER

Heavenly Father, thank you for sending your Son Jesus to be our substitute and to take the judgment I deserved. Write on my heart today a deeper knowledge of all that Jesus's death and resurrection means for me: fullness, strength, faith, wellness, satisfaction, holiness.

Amen

A HIGHER CALLING

BEN JACK

Ben Jack was the Higher Tour Manager for Higher Manchester, and is now a national evangelist for The Message Trust, and manager of Advance: The Message Evangelists Movement.

When I joined the Message Trust in December 2014 to take up position as the Higher Tour Manager, I knew that the journey ahead had the potential to be exciting, challenging and life-changing in equal measure. This was no doubt a race worth running, bringing the opportunity to see thousands of young people impacted by the gospel. Flash forward sixteen months to the climax of Higher Manchester, and we had now seen 30,000 young people in 55 high-schools and 23 youth projects across Greater Manchester during four weeks of intensive outreach. We had welcomed 7,000 young people into the O2 Manchester Apollo for four evangelistic concerts and a celebration event. And, most amazingly of all, we witnessed more than 2,000 young people make a decision to follow Jesus and make him Lord of their lives.

Here at the end of this Higher Manchester journey I was starting to realise just how special this adventure had actually been. Then it hit me – this wasn't the end of the race at all, this was in fact just the beginning....

Speaking of beginnings, perhaps in the interests of good storytelling we should rewind to the start of the Higher journey, a journey which began many months before I had the pleasure of joining the party. Throughout 2014 Andy Hawthorne had received multiple prophetic words around Isaiah 60. This remarkable passage of scripture opens with the words 'Arise, shine, for your light has come, and the glory of the Lord rises upon you', before going on to speak of God's provision and saving work. The passage concludes, 'The least of you will become a thousand, the smallest a mighty nation. I am the Lord; in its time I will do this swiftly' (Isaiah 60:1;22. NIV).

Ben; Higher Manchester 2016; an Advance evangelist group

After much prayer, Andy felt like the Lord was saying that the time was right to 'put the lamp on the stand' once more – to go big and bold with the kind of high-profile evangelistic outreach to young people that The Message was founded on 25 years ago, but that we had not undertaken on such a large scale for more than a decade. Around this time, we also became aware at The Message of some research in the realm of social science known as the 'cultural tipping point'. The theory goes that if just ten percent of a people group holds an unshakeable belief, that belief will likely be adopted by the majority.

We began to ask the question: What would it take to present the gospel to enough young people around the UK that once received and truly lived, it could initiate that kind of cultural change? What if we could see a genuine cultural tipping point achieved in this nation's youth, moving a broken generation back to the wholeness of relationship with their Heavenly Father?

If you are in any doubt that this generation (and nation) needs transformation, let me point you in the direction of a couple of shocking statistics. In Britain one in

ten young people suffer from a clinically diagnosable mental health problem, and tragically, suicide has now become one of the biggest causes of death amongst teenagers in the UK, and the single biggest killer of men and women between the ages of 20-34.

The answer we came up with was to attempt to preach the gospel to two million young people over a five-year period in the hope that 200,000 would receive it and go on to live fully for Christ. This, according to our admittedly basic maths skills, would result in 10% of young people in high schools around the UK following Christ. With him at work in their lives they would then be able to effect a genuine cultural change in their generation, and in this nation, for the glory of God.

So, over a 16-month period we set to work planning and delivering Higher Manchester, a complex outreach to schools and five ambitious concerts at the well-known Apollo. Our creative teams and partner mission bands were the spearhead of the mission, delivering lessons, assemblies and mini-concerts as they travelled from school to school, youth group to youth group. We may never know the full impact of these engagements upon the lives of many of the young people we encountered along the way to the Apollo concerts, but through faithful sharing of testimony and basic explanation of what Christians believe, we continue to pray and believe that those planted seeds will take root and could one day be brought to life.

The concerts themselves were a combination of hugely ambitious music, light, and video productions, with testimonies and a clear presentation of the gospel the primary focus of each night. As young people responded to the invitation to follow Jesus, they were then talked through how to connect with a local church, and their details were gathered so that follow-up could begin quickly to plug them into discipleship courses and a local Christian community.

On March 20 2016, we held the final event of Higher Manchester at the Apollo. This celebration gig was an opportunity for churches from across the region to gather together to hear about all that God had done through Higher, and worship him as one church at the climax of the mission. Worship is the aim of mission – that people would be moved from death to devotion – so what better way to bring this phase of Higher to a close?

AMAZING...

In many ways it is hard to describe just how amazing it was to be involved in the first run of Higher, and to see firsthand what God did through it. You've already read the statistics, but let's be honest, unless you are a stats geek, stories are far more interesting

and insightful as to how God was at work through the mission....

Stories like Tyler's: a young man who was addicted to marijuana and had been excluded not only from school, but from his exclusion provision. Tyler came along to Higher on his own, searching for a little hope as his life was spiralling out of control. He left the Apollo on the Friday night having made a decision to follow Jesus, smashing his marijuana grinder on the floor and replacing it in his pocket with a Bible.

Stories like Adele's, who after a life of addiction and finding temporary love in all the wrong places, accepted Jesus as Lord and felt like a new creation.

Stories like the hundreds of other young people from all sorts of different backgrounds – from addicts and those desperately seeking, to those who were living in comfort seemingly without need for anything – who heard the good news and were all compelled to respond to Jesus and make him Lord of their lives.

Stories like the teacher and youth workers who brought kids along only to receive Jesus themselves. Like the St John's Ambulance worker who heard the gospel message, realised this 'full life' he was hearing about wasn't just for the young people, and responded there and then. And there was the 83-year-old lady who jumped to her feet on the final night when the question 'Do you want to live?' was asked from the stage, and with tears in her eyes said 'I do! I want life! Where can I get a Bible?'

Only the God of that Bible, the God who saves, restores, and transforms could be behind all that we saw during Higher Manchester in 2016. As great as the shows at the Apollo may have been (and the stage productions were pretty epic!), no one who left the events truly transformed and saved by faith did so because of that. They left that way because the gospel was prioritised and proclaimed, and because God who is mighty to save keeps his promises (e.g. Deuteronomy 7:9; Romans 10:9-15).

It's never just about statistics. It's never just about hands in the air as the preacher offers the invitation. It is about individual lives transformed by the power of the gospel. The Living Word has given us stories of life, hope and restoration that we can more than simply report upon – we can humbly and joyfully turn them back to worship.

LEGACY...

A constant theme during the development of Higher was legacy. Our desire has been to see this ambitious youth mission produce disciples, not just decisions. Sometimes large-scale evangelistic outreach can focus so heavily on the *preaching* of the gospel, that we forget about the *living out* of the gospel. This will not do. The legacy of such a mission must be that the young people we evangelise would take this faith and run with it in such a way that this world would never be the same again. The tipping point theory only comes to life if the young people who respond to the gospel are truly transformed by it and carry their 'unshakeable belief' into every area of their life.

Legacy is about handing something down, the passing on of a gift. One analogy that is sometimes used to explain this is the baton passing that takes place within a relay race. This image is helpful to an extent when thinking about evangelism; during the outreach we pass on the gift of the gospel to all who have ears to hear it. However, if we get too heavily entrenched into the mindset of 'passing on the baton', we are at risk of our own running coming to a stop once the baton has been passed, our job seemingly completed.

Recent research suggests that the post-school environment can be a tricky place for a Christian young person (no matter how long they have been a believer) to hold onto their faith. Whilst the apocalyptic numbers of those losing their faith at university have been somewhat exaggerated, there is clearly a challenge for young people when they step out of the comfortable surroundings of home and weekly church engagement and into the big wide world of ideas and the various culture clashes found at university (or any other area of post-school life).

Christian apologist Frank Turek suggests that we are letting our young people down when we send them off to university from youth groups that have never seriously engaged in deep discipleship:

It's not so much that Christian minds are lost at college—it's that Christian minds rarely get to college... many parents and churches emphasise emotion and ignore the biblical commands to develop the mind, which means that most kids skip off to college equipped with nothing more than feel-good emotionalism... What you win kids with, you win them to. If you win them with emotion, you win them to emotion.[i]

Are we reaching our young people with more than just emotion? Importantly, I believe this question actually pre-dates the discipleship task and strikes at the heart of our evangelism itself. What gospel are we preaching? Through Higher we set out to preach the full, unapologetic, transformational gospel of Jesus Christ. A gospel that says: you are not your own, you had chosen death instead of life, but because of Christ's saving work on the cross and his resurrection you can die to your old life and be reborn in the new through faith in him (Romans 3:21-31; 2 Corinthians 5:17).

THE KINGDOM ADVANCES…

The question of what gospel we are actually preaching was firmly in Andy's mind during the development of Higher. As a faithful and uncompromising preacher of the gospel for more than two decades, Andy felt that one of the best ways he could now use his time was to invest in a group of younger evangelists, to mentor, sharpen, encourage and hold them to account for the lives they live and the gospel they preach.

Andy gathered twelve younger preaching evangelists around himself in January 2015 to begin monthly meetings and retreat together once a year. Through the group the gathered evangelists receive teaching, sharpen each other through discussion, and share openly about where they are at in their personal walk with Jesus. The evangelists in the group send emails and text updates about the opportunities and engagements they have to preach the gospel, and encourage each other with the fruit from these opportunities.

The really exciting part of this initiative is that after one year in the group, each evangelist is then challenged to find another twelve evangelists who they then mentor in the same way. This is about evangelists developing evangelists, to see a huge increase around the UK (and beyond) in the number of preaching evangelists who will unashamedly put the lamp on a stand. Imagine the initial groups of twelve expanding over the coming years to become a mighty and numerous collective of evangelists who take the good news to the nations…. Something about that sounds familiar!

On a personal note, I'm embarrassed to say that when Andy first approached me about joining the group I initially turned him down! Whilst I had clearly felt called to evangelism through the preceding decade and had followed that calling, I was now wondering if I was moving into more of a teaching ministry. I was halfway through a Master's degree in Theology at the time and many of my speaking engagements had become more about equipping believers than preaching to the lost.

But thankfully after some prayer and reflection I realised that joining the group was actually a great opportunity in itself to discern whether I was still called to full-time evangelism, and so I eventually signed up. It might sound over the top, but looking back now I believe it would have been one of the biggest mistakes of my life to have missed this opportunity, and my evangelistic ministry sky-rocketed over the following months. Through the time spent in the group (among other things) God has so kindly revealed to me afresh the firm calling upon my life to preach the gospel as an absolute priority and vocation.

It all started with Andy gathering twelve. Eighteen months later we had just over a hundred evangelists gathered at our first conference for the movement, and we now had a name – Advance. Moving forward we believe Advance will continue to grow, with groups multiplying around the globe with a single focus – the equipping of the evangelist to preach the gospel in season and out (2 Timothy 4:1-5).

DISCIPLES, NOT JUST DECISIONS...

After ensuring we are preaching the full gospel, our attention returns once again to the theme of *legacy* and the reality of discipleship. Post-outreach, we must connect these new believers into Christian community where they can grow in a lifelong journey of discipleship. This is often a challenging part of any outreach, and we decided to make us of technology to aid us in the task through the development of the Higher Tour mobile app. The app was designed to connect young people we met in school to the concert nights, but even more importantly, to connect them to local churches who signed up to have their details (including when and where the follow-up meetings would be) included in the app.

We also developed discipleship resources with other agencies such as Youth for Christ and Light, to help local churches begin the discipleship journey with these new believers. Like the evangelistic task itself, in discipleship we must ensure that we are not slipping into a comfortable emotionalism, with the aim of simply 'retaining' young people in church, but actually moving people forward in their faith. Pizza and pool are fine for a social activity, but at what point do we actually engage our young people in a way that impacts the reality of their (often complicated) lives? We must disciple young people in a way that stretches, challenges, and equips them to live out an authentic faith in this complex world. We must not stop running once we win them with the gospel, the race is not over! We continue this race *with* them, we run on *together*. Donald English reminds us that this message is found at the core of Jesus' call upon a person's life:

The discipleship significance is underlined by Jesus' command to those who would follow to take up their cross too (Mark 8:34–38). This is the true path of discipleship, not the permanently clear, bright and shining way but the lowly path of service, or rejection, or persecution, discovering daily the joy that is found not necessarily in happy circumstances but in faithful service and daily rising with him.[ii]

Discipleship is not glamourous. It is hard and costly, yet essential if this transformational gospel is to be revealed as authentic. Those who follow Jesus must be given the tools to withstand the attacks, persecution and daily grind that threaten to choke out the growing faith within their life (Matthew 13:3-8). This doesn't mean that you can't have fun in youth groups, or that there isn't immense joy to be found in the process, but that the pursuit of fun and emotional satisfaction *above all else* and at the cost of deeper engagement will most likely lead to a spiritually and intellectually deficient follower of Jesus who is ill-equipped to withstand the often hostile world they will encounter and dwell within as life progresses.

...let us run with perseverance the race marked out for us, fixing our eyes on Jesus, the pioneer and perfecter of faith. For the joy set before him he endured the cross, scorning its shame, and sat down at the right hand of the throne of God. Consider him who endured such opposition from sinners, so that you will not grow weary and lose heart. (Hebrews 12:1-3, NIV)

When we grow weary, when we want to stop, when we are tempted to settle for the easy route in our own lives, in evangelism, and in the discipling of our young people, let us consider *he who endured* and in doing so not lose heart. Perhaps a better word to describe the hope for Higher (and Advance for that matter) is not legacy but *endurance*. How do we endure together as followers of Jesus at any stage of the race, that we would continue to honour God with our lives, to see others come to know him, and to finish the race well (2 Timothy 4:7)?

That is ultimately what Higher is about – the church of Jesus Christ running *together* so that the baton of faith is passed again and again to as many people as possible, that we would endure until such a time as God himself sees fit for us to cross the finish line.

Having spent a significant amount of time reflecting upon and learning from the first Higher mission, we now believe the time

is right to begin rolling out these city-wide tours across the nation and begin the five-year mission to see a genuine cultural change around the UK.

What a privilege to partner with God in what he is doing in this world! Through missional opportunities such as the Higher Tour, and the evangelistic focus and gospel integrity being championed by Advance, it really is an exciting time to be involved with The Message Trust as we attempt to faithfully step into the calling and vision that God has given us. And so in his strength, we continue to run....

For more on the Higher Tour, visit: highertour.com

For more on the Advance Evangelist Movement visit: message.org.uk/advance

---

[i] From *Stealing From God: Why Atheists Need God To Make Their Case* by Frank Turek

[ii] From *The Bible Speaks Today: The Message Of Mark* by Donald English

RIVERS IN THE DESERT

CHAPTER FOUR

ISAIAH 43:18-21

'Forget the former things;

    do not dwell on the past.

See, I am doing a new thing!

    Now it springs up; do you not perceive it?

I am making a way in the wilderness

    and streams in the wasteland.

The wild animals honour me,

    the jackals and the owls,

because I provide water in the wilderness

    and streams in the wasteland,

to give drink to my people, my chosen,

    the people I formed for myself

    that they may proclaim my praise.'

Isaiah 43:18-21

"

I'm so grateful that God gave us these verses as our touchstone verses because they contain everything I want The Message to be, and to become

This chapter of Isaiah is foundational in The Message's history. Perhaps you know the story already; perhaps you don't. In 1987, my brother Simon and I had the idea for the first Message event, 'Message 88', which was to become the biggest youth mission Manchester had ever seen. We'd had this idea of booking the Apollo for the week, partnering with the local church on hundreds of local missions, with a special focus on the hardest to reach. But after having the idea, and having gone back home all excited about hearing from God, every ounce of faith drained out of us. I sat on my bed and said 'God, if this really is you... if you want us to step out in this, we haven't got the vast amount of money it's going to cost... we haven't got the connections, nobody knows us, we're just two young lads with a vision. Lord, will you please speak to me through your Word?'. Well, my set reading for that day was Isaiah 43 – I was doing one of these Bible in a Year things – and once I'd read the verses for the day, I immediately phoned Simon and said, 'God's going to do this, Si'.

The verses were Isaiah 43:18-21, '*Forget the former things, do not dwell on the past. See, I'm doing a new thing, now it springs up; do you not perceive it? I'm making a way in the wilderness and streams in the wasteland. The wild animals honour me, the jackals and the owls, because I provide water in the wilderness and streams in the wasteland to give drink to my people, my chosen, the people I formed for myself that they may proclaim my praise*'.

We put those verses on the bottom of our first letterhead, wrote to every church in Manchester and in lots of ways, in all these years, we haven't left those verses. I love the way God speaks to us through his Word and keep revealing things new things through it, keeps taking us forward through his revelation.

Sometimes it's good to just go back and make sure we're still on track with what God's said. That's why I'm so grateful that God gave us these verses as our touchstone verses because they contain everything I want The Message to be, and to become. Everything God's planned for us I believe is in these verses. We're not going to stay put, we're going to keep coming back to them because firstly it says 'forget the former things, don't dwell in the past'. But God is saying to every believer, for every day, 'See, can you see? See, I'm doing new things'.

Prayer, presence and proclamation

These same verses took on new meaning to me when I watched a video of the Negev Desert being flooded. The Negev Desert takes up over half of Israel in landmass and it's one of the driest places on Earth. Things don't grow there until something happens, until there's rain in the mountains. Every now and again, people will see the rain in the distance, in the mountains, and they'll know that life is going to come flowing down from the mountains, they know rivers are going to flow and suddenly – soon afterwards – everyone's got water to drink and things are growing. People gather together as they know it happens very rarely but when it does there's a party going on.

I was really excited when I saw the video because that's the very place where Bible history happened. This is where Abraham wandered, and the children of Israel wandered for their 40 years, the very place it was prophesied that there will be 'rivers in the desert' and they can come very quickly when things shift. When things shift on high the rivers can flow very, very quickly.

Watching that video, I got an overwhelming sense that life-giving water is going to flow again in our nation once we see three things in place; three things in the mountains, if you like, that are going to affect the people in the dry and arid places. As I wrote in the introduction to my first book of teaching from Isaiah (*Here I Am, Send Me*, 2014), I think they are *prayer*, *presence* and *proclamation*.

Far more important than the amount of people who are working for you, the number who come to events, the size of the vision you've got, or how big your budget is, is the temperature of *prayer* in the organisation. That's because prayer affects things 'in the mountains' and before you know it the rivers start to flow down from on high. I'm excited about the prayer temperature here at The Message. We pray together often – every morning, on our monthly Prayer Days and in concentrated times of intercession in the Prayer Room. We prioritise it. We staff for it, with a Prayer Coordinator role. We have helped launch Prayer Storm, a whole movement committed to raising up young intercessors for revival. But we always want more, don't we? I want every single one of us to be on tiptoes of expectation.

When the rain falls in the mountains we're going to see the evidence of that in the schools, prisons and estates through our *presence* there, because prayer that doesn't lead to presence is just piety. God doesn't want Christians locked away in little ivory towers. Our prayer has got to result in presence, people carrying God's blessing out. Through Eden and our work in prisons and with ex-offenders, The Message pours out our lives into young men and women from the margins.

But we don't stop there. Presence needs to turn into clear *proclamation* of the gospel. If we remove the proclamation what are we all about? What have we got left if we actually take the gospel that changes lives and changes communities out of it? God has called us to bold proclamation too – the impetus behind the Higher Tour.

A river of life hits the desert and life springs up. We're here to be rivers in the desert, people who 'give drink to his chosen people' (21), and as far as we're concerned, God has chosen *everybody*. God wants everybody to be saved. We're not going to get worked up about 'are they chosen or are they not' – we're just going to love everybody because the Bible says that God wants all people to be saved. All people should get a drink from this river of life-giving water.

I believe as we pray, as we presence, as we proclaim, we will see 'wild animals honour God', people whose lives were utterly chaotic. I love taking our MEC team members to business dinners and fund-raisers, to let them share their stories. I recently travelled to London with Laura Wilding from our Shine Hair & Beauty business. As she spoke I just sat there thinking 'Jesus, you are amazing!' How can somebody go from utter brokenness, injecting heroin, shattered, her kid taken off her, sectioned, into this beautiful woman of God we see working for us in Shine Hair & Beauty? Nobody else can do that but Jesus!

Focus on the poor

I got an email yesterday asking why there is such a strong focus on the poor, hurting and tougher estates in our work. 'Why do you spend so much time going into prisons? What about nice people? What about all these nice people who need Jesus?' Well, I'll tell you why: because I honestly believe that it's Jesus' heart and Jesus' focus. Jesus loves everybody of course, but there's a gospel imperative in the Bible to go to the poor, the marginalised and the hurting. We can't get away from the inordinate amount of time Jesus spent on demoniacs, lepers, prostitutes, gang members and tax collectors. He just surrounded himself with them, poured his life into the most hurting.

But his strategy wasn't just for them – his strategy was for the whole world to be saved. When you see transformation come amongst the most broken, the most hurting, the most vulnerable, it changes society and everyone gets blessed. Our vision is for whole cities to be saved, but we're not going to do that on our own. We're going to start where God has told us to start. Every bit of evidence down history points to the fact that if there's going to be a revival, we need to start on the margins. If we can see prisons emptied and crime coming down, the whole city will be blessed. And that's going to bring great glory to Jesus. This is what we're called to.

REFLECTION

1. Do you have a 'life verse', or a scripture that you keep coming back to through the different seasons of your life?

2. Prayer is where it all begins – the place from which the rain falls 'in the mountains'. Are you giving enough time to prayer?

3. Would you spend some time praying for The Message today? Ask God to give us new measures of favour in our work in schools, communities and prisons.

PRAYER

Lord Jesus, help me to see the 'new thing' you are doing in me and around me today.

Amen

TESTIMONY:
CYRIL WILDING

'God's not just turned my life around, he's transformed me'

Andy adds: After years of drug and sexual abuse Cyril Wilding's life was at its lowest point when he ended up on suicide watch while in prison. But his life was turned around when a brave old lady visited him and told him about Jesus. Now Cyril works as our Facilities Assistant and uses every opportunity he can to tell others how Jesus has transformed his life. He's amazing.

As a 12-year-old my childhood was snatched from me when I started being sexually abused. This went on for two years and I just could not handle the pain I was going through.

At the age of 13 I started drinking alcohol to numb the pain. I was 14 when I first tried drugs, which was LSD. It gave me the feeling of pleasure that my life wasn't giving me, and my answer was to get out of my face, often. All my money went on drink and drugs and I would rob anyone who came across my path to pay for it.

By the time I left my teens I was a full-blown addict. Probably one of the worst going, in fact. I was going weeks without properly sleeping, because I was taking so much speed and coke.

After leaving home in Wigan I tried to make a fresh start but somehow I ended up in gang and car crime, selling drugs on the streets of Manchester to fund my drug habit. I thought I was a big man but I was wrecking other people's lives and I was wrecking my own.

By the age of 30, my whole life was in pieces. Drugs and drink were not taking the pain away any more so I had turned to self-harm. There I was, 30 years old, sitting in a corner crying, depressed, cutting myself with a blade because I was so unhappy with my life. I was desperate for love.

Thank God Jesus met me. It was about ten years ago during my last prison sentence in Forest Bank prison. I was on what was called a '20-52', which is a suicide watch. The prison officers thought I was going to end my life and to be honest, they were right. That's what I was going to do.

That was until a little old lady came into my pad. She told me that Jesus died for me all the pain I was carrying about, he put on the cross for me. I thought she was a nut job at first! But when she left I opened up the Bible and discovered it was true. I read Psalm 23 with new eyes. I heard him say to me that he was all I needed. I knew this was the love I was looking for. So that day, I asked Jesus to come into my life. Straightaway I could feel a change in my heart. I lost the desire to do drugs and the self-harm stopped too.

At the lowest point in my life I got support from Victory Outreach Manchester. They helped me put my life back together, depending on Jesus day by day. I met an amazing woman of God, Laura, and we got married.

I now work at The Message as a Facilities Assistant looking after the buildings and the cars on site.

(Clockwise from top left): at work at The Message; with wife, Laura and others from the Message Enterprise Centre volunteer prisons team; sharing his story at Higher Manchester 2016; grateful to God for new life

I love the variety and challenges of the job, but I also appreciate how you can get anybody to pray for you when I'm going through a difficult time. There are people who've been through the same stuff I've been through so they can understand the challenges I'm facing at times.

Myself and a colleague also put together an outreach team of people who work at the MEC called Message on the Move. The first place we went to was Forest Bank Prison, which is the same prison I got saved in. Amazingly 27 people committed their lives to Christ that day. Now every month we go to a soup kitchen for the homeless in Rochdale, as well as going into prisons and schools.

At the recent Higher night, I got the chance to share my story with over two thousand young people at the O₂ Apollo Manchester. Looking out at all their faces, I remembered how it felt to be 14 again. I felt compassion for them all, because my life was already a mess by then. But I could tell them there is hope for them all because God has done something amazing in me.

I told them I'm not a drug addict or an alcoholic any more. I told them that even though my arms are scarred I'm not ashamed any more. Because there's someone who's set me free and his name is Jesus.

And when the gospel was preached later that night, it made me so happy to see hundreds of young people putting up their hands to respond. To know that they had heard the same thing I did – there is hope and his name is Jesus.

It's great that my wife Laura also works at the Message Trust at the MEC's Shine hair and beauty salon. What's even more special though is that we both get the chance to go out and minister together.

God's not just turned my life around, he's transformed me. I used to see myself as being this victim to drugs, alcohol and abuse, but now I'm a survivor. I only survived through God. But it's good to go out and give hope to other people who are going through what I went through.

Now I wake up every single day and the first thing I do is I thank him. It was him that gave me my life back. I owe him everything.

THE
ANOINTING
OF GOD

CHAPTER FIVE

'This is what the Lord says to his anointed…

I will go before you and will level the mountains;

I will break down gates of bronze and cut through bars of iron.

I will give you hidden treasures, riches stored in secret places,

so that you may know that I am the Lord,

the God of Israel, who summons you by name.

For the sake of Jacob my servant, of Israel my chosen,

I summon you by name and bestow on you a title of honour,

though you do not acknowledge me.

I am the Lord, and there is no other;

apart from me there is no God.

I will strengthen you,

though you have not acknowledged me,

so that from the rising of the sun

to the place of its setting

people may know there is none besides me.

I am the Lord, and there is no other.'

Isaiah 45:1-6

"

What would happen if the church truly became what it was meant to be?

I realise that I'm a bit old to be saying this but I really love Christian hip-hop artist Lecrae. He's been number one recently in the mainstream charts in the U.S.

I watched him on the biggest syndicated hip-hop show in America recently and he really stood up for Christ. They talked to him about groupies and said, 'Lecrae, you're making a lot of money now – number one in all the charts, how do you cope when all these girls start flinging themselves at you?' which is a good question to ask of a Christian, isn't it? Lecrae replied, 'The way I look at it, Nissan have a big marketing budget because their cars aren't that amazing, and so they have to advertise a lot. Whereas Ferrari hardly spend any money advertising because everyone knows they're the best and you have to go and chase them down. They are the type of ladies I find more attractive, those who don't advertise themselves – they're so beautiful that you have to chase them down'.

As he was saying this, I thought: isn't that true of the church as well? If we became what we were truly meant to be, we wouldn't need to advertise – people would be chasing us down. They'd want to know: 'What is going on in that place? How is it that people are getting healed, set free, delivered, growing; becoming beautiful, generous, gracious people?'

Isaiah 45 paints a wonderful picture of that kind of breakthrough happening. It's what we long for, it's what The Message is all about, it's called *revival*. And Isaiah 45 gives us a glimpse into what will be involved in that transformation – when the church becomes the beautiful bride she was meant to be.

An anointed people

We need the anointing of God: I need it, you need it. The passage starts by saying '*this is what the Lord says to the anointed, to Cyrus...*' and suddenly here's a new character taking central stage. Israel's in disarray and they need a man anointed by God. Cyrus was the deliverer, the king who was going to set the people free. In the Old Testament, 'the anointing' means the Holy Spirit coming on somebody so that in their flesh they can do things that fleshly people could never do. That's what it means to be anointed, for God to come upon you. In the Old Testament God used to come upon men like Cyrus, often at disastrous times in the nation's history when they were in disarray.

Here we are, in the UK which is, in lots of ways, in disarray too. It's crazy what's happening to our young people and more than ever we need to be an anointed people. In the Old Testament the anointing came and it was limited and temporary – it came for a season. But now it's liberal and permanent. We are meant to be truly anointed of God. It's something that's available to every single believer. It that means you can do the things you could never do in your flesh and it means you can fulfil your God-given purpose. Because you have a purpose, something you were made for purpose and the anointing of God enables you to fulfil the full measure of that purpose. We need people who are carrying the anointing 24/7, don't we?

It's something we need, to overcome our addictions, to overcome our phobias and fears, to overcome our sins which hold us back. Lots of us will know this famous scripture: '*We have this treasure, the Holy Spirit, the anointing of God in jars of clay to show this all-surpassing power is from God and not from us*' (2 Corinthians 4:7). And I love this from 1 John 2, too: '*You have an anointing from the holy one ... as for you, the anointing you received from him remains in you... as his anointing teaches you about all things and as that anointing is real not counterfeit, just as it has been taught you, remain in him*' (20, 27).

Do you want to know what the secret is to being an anointed man or woman of God, full to overflowing with the Holy Spirit, doing things in your flesh that fleshly people could never do? Do you want to know what the secret is? Let me tell you; remain in him! You can't remove the anointing from the Anointed One. Do you want to be a person who when you preach the gospel, when you share about Jesus, extraordinary things happen? When you lay hands on the sick more people than ever get healed? When you pray for those who are broken God's power breaks in? Someone who in their own life is walking in victory – do you want to be that kind of person? Well, remain in him! Go after the Anointed One! Get to know Jesus! Spend time with Jesus! Fall in love with Jesus! In other words, as it's been said so often; 'seek the giver, not the gift'.

What only he can do

The truth is, we need God to do the things that only he can do. Unless God breaks in, unless God chooses to use that and display his glory through us we're stuffed aren't we? Listen to this: '*I will level the mountains, break down the gates of bronze and cut through the bars of iron*' (2). It's a picture of God doing the things that only he can do; levelling mountains, breaking down impossible barriers. There's no obstacle too great for God so that we can fulfil his purpose for our lives. There's no man, no government, no scheme of hell that has an obstacle too great that God can't flatten in a moment. We can't see heroin addicts set free and families restored in our own strength. We can't see people who all they've known is crime suddenly on a different path, drug dealers dealing death suddenly dealing hope... but God can. He's about mountain-levelling breakthrough, our God who helps us break through impossible barriers.

Isaiah 45 speaks of an anointed people, and we're not going to do what we need to do without the anointing of God. It speaks of a people who depend on God doing the things that only he can do even if we've got all the anointing in the world. And it speaks of a people who keep the uniqueness of Christ central. Listen to these verses: '*I am the Lord and apart from me there is no other*' (5), '*I am the Lord and there is no other*' (6), '*I am the Lord and I do all these things*' (7). Do you get the picture? There's only one God, there's only one Lord and we can't back down from that. He's the Way, the Truth and the Life. Nobody gets to God except through him. It's an offence to some but we've got to keep the uniqueness of Christ at the centre because with all the anointing in the world, unless we lift high the name of Jesus we're never going to do what we're meant to do.

Of course we love others, we operate in grace, we don't look to pick unnecessary fights – but we have to lift high the name of Jesus because Jesus is the only hope, he is the Lord! We have an inclusive gospel that's for all people, that works for every person, but they only find their purpose through the exclusiveness of Christ. It's for everybody but it's all in him.

There's no formula for revival but there is a *foundation* upon which God always builds revival. Without that foundation we're not going to see it happen. We don't know when suddenly, God's going to do the things that he can do. The formula is God's, that's down to God. But I believe the foundation is down to us. In our lives, if we chase after Jesus, if we fight sin, if we believe in the miraculous, if we believe for the breakthrough and we keep Jesus central, then when God is ready we'll be part of the action..

And my burning desire is to say 'oh, God, you've given us so many promises, please, before I die and go to be with Jesus, will you let us see this massive harvest?' We're going to keep going, keep chasing, keep loving, keep serving, keep praying because at any moment the breakthrough could come.

REFLECTION

1. In what ways do you think the church would be more attractive to the world if it were all God intended it to be?

2. How have you personally experienced the anointing of God? In what ways do you crave more of the Lord's anointing?

3. Ask God to fill you to overflowing with his Holy Spirit – that you would bring breakthrough to the people and situations around you.

PRAYER

Holy Spirit, I ask you to fill me to overflowing today. I want to carry the anointing of Jesus into every area of my life and I need your help to do it.

Amen

'I'm so thankful
that God has given
me an opportunity
to save other lives'

My brother and I were brought up by our mum on an estate in Collyhurst Village, Manchester. It was a rough area but my mum did her best. My dad was hardly ever around when I was growing up. From the age of 11 I got into drink. We used to go to the shops during school breaks and buy alcohol and then it continued out of school.

In time, I got into drugs and became addicted to speed and cocaine. I left home when I was just 17. To pay my rent and feed my addiction, I was doing anything to make some money including dealing drugs, selling stolen goods and looking after guns for people. I also worked in hospitals doing the laundry on night shifts. But as my addiction continued I got into a lot of debt and I was constantly dodging drug dealers I owed money to. It got so bad that I actually spent my 18th birthday in a police cell for beating my mum up because she wouldn't give me money for drugs.

I tried to overcome my addiction by moving away to Blackpool where I worked in a hotel. But I was feeling very low and had no friends to turn to at all.

On two occasions I even tried to end my life by jumping off the pier, but each time someone stopped me. I now believe that this was God intervening in my life.

My dad would just come visit me from time to time throughout my childhood and give me a present or money and I remember calling him from Blackpool. For the first time he told me he loved me and I started breaking down.

After about a year I moved back to Manchester and worked at a gambling arcade where I would give people change for the slot machines and that's where I met my husband, Nick. He was also on drugs at the time, and he was a drug dealer and a gambler. I was living in a basement and Nick had nowhere to stay, so he came to stay with me and he never left.

At the time I was still on drugs and Nick was dealing drugs and smoking weed. We used to fight a lot and one time he came home beaten up because drug dealers had taken his drugs off him. I was still on cocaine when I found out I was pregnant with my daughter Alexis. I never took it again.

Then suddenly a miracle happened: Nick became a Christian and just wouldn't stop talking to me about God and the Bible. For me having a drug dealer boyfriend to someone talking about God all the time – well, I thought he'd lost the plot. What really changed him was when he started working at The Message Trust. He knew Andy Hawthorne from years before and he'd gone to see him saying that he'd do anything, including clean the toilets, just to get into evangelism ministry. What was crazy was I

(Clockwise from top left): in Uganda with CRMI Children of Hope;
sharing hope at Higher Manchester 2016; Uganda; with family in Manchester, UK

remembered the World Wide Message Tribe coming to my school when I was about 11 – that was probably when a seed was first sown in me. I didn't put my hand up. What we didn't realise till later was that while Andy was coming to my school he was doing the same with Nick.

What really turned me around was when I met Jane Sullivan at the Message in 2011. Nick introduced me to her in the prayer room one day. After chatting for a while she asked me if I knew who Jesus was. I said no, I didn't. She told me about God's love for me in a nice calm way. I froze when she said he could be like my father. She told me that this Father would never let me down. So I gave my life to the Lord in that prayer room.

Then she told me about the charity she was working for, CRMI Children of Hope, and she asked me if I wanted to go to Uganda, which is where I'd always wanted to go to help children. That June we flew out to Uganda on my first mission trip. Just a few months later, Nick and I got married.

My faith changed how I saw Nick. I saw him wanting to be a good father, wanting the best for us because I didn't have that growing up. Also my relationship with my mum changed for the better. My dad passed away two years ago. A year after the wedding before he died I was able to introduce him to my daughter Alexis and he apologised for being absent all those years. I was able to forgive him for keeping his other family life away from me and keeping me a secret from them all those years.

What's amazing is now I've taken over much of the work of Children of Hope.

Since that first mission trip I've not stopped and now go twice a year. I just can't imagine my life without the charity being in it. I treat the children like they're my own. They call me even 'Mama Andrea'. My life used to be all about me, but now I just want to help others and give back.

I'm so thankful that Andy Hawthorne and The Message Trust believed in him. Now he's part of the hip-hop missions team Vital Signs at The Message Trust. I believe this is where I was supposed to be. I'm so thankful that God not only saved my life but he's given me an opportunity to save other lives.

THE CROSS

CHAPTER SIX

ISAIAH 53:1-6

Who has believed our message

   and to whom has the arm of the Lord been revealed?

He grew up before him like a tender shoot,

   and like a root out of dry ground.

He had no beauty or majesty to attract us to him,

   nothing in his appearance that we should desire him.

He was despised and rejected by mankind,

   a man of suffering, and familiar with pain.

Like one from whom people hide their faces

   he was despised, and we held him in low esteem.

Surely he took up our pain and bore our suffering,

yet we considered him punished by God, stricken by him, and afflicted.

But he was pierced for our transgressions, he was crushed for our iniquities;

the punishment that brought us peace was on him,

   and by his wounds we are healed.

We all, like sheep, have gone astray,

   each of us has turned to our own way;

and the Lord has laid on him

   the iniquity of us all.

Isaiah 53:1-6

"

When we look at the cross we should never want to sin again

The story is told of Daryl Lumis, a haulage driver in the States. Every week he travelled the same route from Cincinnati to Atlanta with goods on his articulated lorry. Daryl's usual stop-off was Joe's Diner, and he always made sure to call in en route for his favourite – hot meatloaf sandwich and mashed potatoes, with a glass of iced tea.

One afternoon, Daryl parked up his truck as usual and walked into Joe's, sat down at the counter and placed his usual order. Suddenly, with a roar of engines and a massive cloud of dust, twelve fearsome bikers pulled up next to Daryl's truck – a neat line of shiny Harley-Davidsons.

Clearly looking for trouble, the gang swaggered into the diner and approached Daryl, forming a semi-circle behind him. With an air of menace, the leader drew up alongside him. 'Who's the sissy at the counter?' he sneered. Daryl remained silent and continued eating his lunch. Then, to the jeers and taunts of the rest of the gang, one of the bikers picked up Daryl's drink and poured it slowly over his head. Using his napkin, Daryl dried his face but said nothing and just kept on eating.

Still trying to get a reaction from Daryl, another gang member picked up a handful of mashed potatoes and stuck it in Daryl's ear, wiping his hand down the back of his overalls. Still, Daryl remained calm and continued to eat his lunch without a word. When he'd finished his lunch, he stood up slowly and politely paid his bill. 'Thanks, Joe. See you next time.'

Daryl left the diner without even acknowledging the bikers. The leader of the gang laughed loudly and said to Joe behind the counter, 'What a wimp that guy was. He sure ain't much of a man!' From behind the counter, Joe looked out of the window and replied, 'He ain't much of a driver either – he's just run over twelve Harleys!'

I really hope the story's true, don't you? In a funny way, it's a picture of the cross, isn't it? Jesus looked so pathetic, so lame, hanging on the cross – but actually he was destroying Satan. He was destroying our great enemy, sin and death, once and for all. In Isaiah 53 we have classic prophetic words of Christ suffering. In some ways if these were the only prophecies we had it would still be utterly astonishing: 600 years before Jesus even set foot on Earth.

Imagine writing them down, like Isaiah. Imagine if this was your prophetic download from heaven that you have to share before the people... a picture of God himself stricken and smitten, broken and pierced and crushed. Sure, it's not too hard to prophesy about 'the Lord high and lifted up', 'his throne filling the temple' and 'the glory of the Lord'. But can we imagine *this* God? He doesn't sound like much of a God at all, does he? Is it any wonder that at the start of chapter 53, Isaiah says 'Who has believed our message?'?

We preach Christ crucified

Of course, Jesus' own disciples had trouble believing Jesus himself when he turned towards Jerusalem at the start of his Passion. Jesus said 'Everything that is written by the prophets about the son of man will be fulfilled. He'll be handed over to the Gentiles, they'll mock him, insult him, spit on him, flog him and kill him. And on the third day he will rise again.' The disciples just couldn't get it. We'll keep the miracles and the glorious teaching, but we don't get this: he's got to be spat on, flogged, insulted, crucified? But here it is, 600 years before Christ, clearly prophesied that the saviour of the world will be pierced for our transgressions.

It's really exciting that with Advance we could see a viral movement of preaching evangelists. But from the beginning, I've insisted that we ask 'What is the gospel that we preach to produce maximum disciples and not just decisions?'. After all, wouldn't we rather have ten disciples in a school than 500 decisions? The answer is, as Paul puts it, we preach Christ crucified. Sum up the evangelist's job in four words, that's it: we preach Christ crucified.

I still remember, at the end of 1977, recommitting my life to Christ – hearing the message of the cross and going forward for my first communion as a dedicated follower of Christ. In some ways it was quite lame really: a little piece of bread and a little sip of wine, and I'm looking up at a picture of Jesus in a stained glass window and he's got blonde hair and blue eyes, and yet I was just gripped by the cross, I was just captivated. In fact, the first few times I received communion after that I remember being absolutely so grateful to Christ that he would go through that great suffering for me. I was so sorrowful that I'd made a commitment at 12 years old and then almost thrown it in his face, and I hadn't really lived it. I never want to lose that sense of the glory of the cross. I think much of the dualism that we see in the church is because we haven't understood the great price that was paid. It hasn't sunk in that he was really pierced for our sin.

Two incredible blessings

There are two incredible blessings described in Isaiah 53. Firstly, 'the punishment that brought us peace was upon him' (5). Without the cross there is no true peace. The gift to a Christian is peace this world cannot understand, peace that passes understanding. Only Jesus can bring true peace, and isn't it right that with peace a poor man is rich, without peace a rich man is poor? The greatest prize in the universe is peace, peace with each other, peace with God, peace as we look forward to the future and the cross brings peace because it makes us right with God and with our fellow men. Peace. The punishment that bought us peace was on him.

Secondly, 'by his wounds we were healed' (5). What from? From deadly sin sickness. I'm a sinful man and all I deserve is separation from God, all I deserve is hell and rejection. Yet what am I looking forward to? Heaven and eternal life. I'm not sin-sick any more, I haven't got this deadly disease that results in judgement and hell. Instead, because of the cross I've been forgiven. I've taken the only medicine that can heal the sin-sick man: the blood of Jesus.

I think it's right that we should meditate on the physical sufferings of Christ. Some argue that we shouldn't make too much of the physical sufferings. But if we're not meant to make too much of the physical sufferings, how come Jesus chose to die probably the most barbaric death that mankind has ever devised? The Romans were wicked executioners. John Piper says, 'If we had been forced to watch it, we probably would pass out... The victim of crucifixion literally died a thousand deaths.' Crucifixion was the worst, most barbaric death and our Jesus went through it for us. He did it to show how far love can go, but also as a picture of how terrible our sin does. When we look at the cross we should never want to sin again.

We must be changed

Our lives have got to be changed by the cross. Imagine Jesus walking into Jerusalem, and as he walks into Jerusalem there were men hanging on crosses. Some of them would have been screaming for mercy, some of them would have been hallucinating in the pure agony, hanging there, the Romans saying, 'This is how we treat the worst of our criminals', and he's already told his disciples, 'This is how I'm going to die'. Imagine how he felt in that moment: 'In a few hours' time this will be me.'

I believe Jesus' flesh did recoil: he would have had a gut-wrenching, horrible feeling in his stomach. He would have had sweaty palms. In fact, the Bible tells us his sweat was like great drops of blood. Sweating blood is a recognised physical condition at times of extreme mental distress – your pores can open up and literally blood can come out – but I don't think it was the physical agony that was the most terrible thing for Jesus to face; it was the thought of separation. The only one who truly walked with God perfectly. The only person who ever experienced the delight of unhindered access to the Father. Full access, not marred by sin. The one who could say, 'I only do what the Father tells me to do. Me and the Father are one.' He knew that he was going to be abandoned, knew that he was going to be separated. Imagine how that felt to Jesus: that was the thing that truly horrified him.

And what a cry from Jesus' lips. As the sky went black, a historic event, 'My God, my God, why have you abandoned me?' And no answer came. We have the privilege two thousand years later of telling the world the answer to that question, 'My God, my God, why have you abandoned me?'. I'll tell you why: because of his great love for every person who ever lived. Because of his great love for this world, because God wants a people, and somebody has to be punished. Without the shedding of blood there's no forgiveness; somebody had to take the rap.

The natural consequence of understanding the cross is that your knee bows, your tongue exalts him, and your life is laid down for others. If we get it, if we have any understanding of Jesus' great sacrifice for us, it's got to change the way we live.

REFLECTION

1. 'Crushed for my iniquity'.... Meditate for a few minutes on the blessings that are yours because Jesus was nailed to the cross.

2. Contemplate the two 'incredible blessings' of verse 5. How do you realise them in your life?

3. How do you think a clearer picture of the cross should change our mission, our discipleship, our attitudes to suffering?

PRAYER

'Heaven is too great, hell is too horrible, eternity is too long that we should potter around on the porch of eternity. Oh God open our eyes to the vastness of the sufferings of Christ and what they may mean for sin and holiness.' (John Piper)

Lord, make us awake to the weight of glory, the glory of Christ in comparable sufferings, in his great and wonderful name,

Amen

WELCOME HOME
LINDA MCKAY

Linda McKay joined The Message as an administrator in 2015. She moved into The Oaks in March 2016, and from January 2017 she will be the full-time Chaplain for our Message Enterprise Centre.

Over the past ten years I have lived on three continents, preaching the gospel in over 20 nations and loving some of the most marginalised communities on earth. AIDS-stricken townships and desert border towns within earshot of a warzone have been my home, and garbage dumps, refugee camps and red-light districts have been my office.

At the beginning of 2015 I was sitting on a rooftop in Jordan drinking coffee, when I felt Jesus calling me back to the UK. After almost two years of living and working amongst Syrian refugees it was time to 'help sow seeds of Oaks of Righteousness' in the UK. At the time I has no idea what he meant by that. By that evening I had applied for an office-based job with The Message Trust, an organisation I knew very little about, but one whose vision I was willing to serve.

I stepped off the plane and into another of those great Jesus stories. Two hours after landing back in Manchester I was sitting in an interview. A week later I was signing a contract. A year on, I embarked on my next adventure – moving into The Oaks.

The Oaks – a building that 'just happened' to be purchased the month I arrived back in the UK – is a 12-bedroom house just a short drive away from our Message Enterprise Centre, offering a residential support programme to men and women who want to leave the chaos of broken lives strewn with addiction and offending behind them in exchange for an abundant life marked with peace, joy and righteousness.

Over the past four years, the MEC has seen great success in lives being transformed. We have helped over 40 young people through vocational training and jobs in our four businesses. In that time fewer than 10% have reoffended, and over 70%

Linda; The Oaks; Simon and Jane Sullivan

are now in employment, either with us or elsewhere. Considering over 60% of prison leavers are normally back behind bars within two years, this is a remarkable result. The Oaks is another step in building on that success. Until now we have been able to offer training, employment, housing and discipleship. The opening of The Oaks means we can now offer a family for those not yet ready for employment or independent living.

I arrived just as the dream of The Oaks was starting to became reality, and in doing so I stepped into a tale spanning over 40 years; one rich with God's miraculous guidance, favour and provision. It's a tale that starts with a house being given by the Queen to a girl in need of safety and security, and finishes with a house being provided by the King of Kings for guys who, too, need just that.

Simon Sullivan and his wife Jane sold the house they had called home for 25 years to move into the heart of Wythenshawe with their teenage son to be our live-in leaders at The Oaks. It was a move that Simon had vowed he would never make. Simon's mum became pregnant with him as 15-

year old whilst in care. It was at this time that the first house – one just around the corner from The Oaks – was given as a gift. In a 'moment of madness', Simon's mum, desperate for some safety and security for her and her new son, wrote to the Queen pleading for help. Much to her surprise, she received a letter back directing her to a local council office where she was told keys for a house were waiting for her. With his dad in prison, Simon spent his earliest (and some of his most difficult) years in Wythenshawe. He recalls, 'I hated Wythenshawe and never ever wanted to go back. It was a place of pain and trauma for me.'

Fast forward 40 years, and Simon and Jane were happily married, raising a family in Stockport and doing some amazing work in our Prisons team, seeing lives transformed by Jesus. But according to Simon, it all started feeling 'too comfortable'. Jane had a feeling that the Lord was leading them back to Wythenshawe and the dream of having a big family home where our team members could put down roots and flourish at the same time as blessing the community started to grip her heart. But for Simon that was still too much. Wythenshawe was a place he was glad to have escaped from, not a place he wanted to raise a family.

Around two years ago, though, things started to change. At a Message Prayer Day the Lord started to clearly speak to both Simon and Jane about them 'returning to his people', much like Moses had done in the book of Exodus. As God spoke, Simon's pain was transformed into compassion. Wythenshawe was in need of Jesus. Simon's heart was broken for the lives gripped by the same pain and trauma that had so marked his early life.

Jesus had Simon and Jane's 'yes', and The Message was fully on board with their vision. When The Oaks – previously a manse, and then a care home owned by a local church in Wythenshawe – came up for sale, there was a feeling of 'rightness' about purchasing it. This was the place. But there was a battle yet to be fought.

Simon and Jane received a word from someone who knew nothing of their dreams, that the Lord had a house for them, a house that would bring immense freedom and salvation, but also that this house had a chain wrapped around it that would be released in 19 months. It was a word that they held on to as plans for the house met roadblocks at every single junction possible. There were outright refusals, and very real and vocal objections by police, councillors and neighbours. At one point they were bluntly instructed, 'Get your deposit back. We aren't going to allow this.' The vision was continually met by scepticism, reticence and much fear, not to mention concerns over the financial implications. Yet time and time again – and particularly as people

came close enough to truly hear the heart behind the house – refusals turned into teary-eyed pledges of full support. The sale was completed 19 months after the word was given. So miraculous was the journey, there were no doubts this was a house provided by the King.

Much like Simon's own journey, fear was sidelined by compassion. It is compassion that helps us look past the dysfunction and see, truly see, the hurting individual underneath. A little while ago, just around the corner from The Oaks, I hugged a homeless guy farewell after I had spent some time sitting in the rain chatting with him about a life plagued by tragedy and addiction. My heart was aching for the lost, the lonely and the hurting in this nation. We don't have to look far to find them if we really choose to see. As I walked away I realised that I stank of stale alcohol. Strangely enough, it made me feel at home – much as the smell of burning rubbish did in Africa, or the tear-induced make-up stains all over my clothes after a night in a red-light district, or the pungency of an afternoon sat on urine-soaked refugee mats. This is where I belong. With the hurting and the broken. It once again reminded that if we want people to smell like us (and the One whose fragrance we carry), we need to be close enough to walk away smelling like them. Their brokenness needs our presentness.

I have a substantial dream list for life. Number 22: Never let anyone feel invisible in my presence. So often, loving starts with choosing to see, and allowing ourselves to be inconvenienced for love's sake. When Jesus commanded us to love, I believe he meant it. Much like our Eden teams, I have always taken a very incarnational approach to mission and ministry. If you want to wage war on hopelessness you can't just talk about the goodness of God, you have to demonstrate it. My 'I love you' needs to be more than just words. Love – like Jesus – comes alongside the broken and says, 'I am here.' Much like the Sullivans, that was my inspiration in moving in to The Oaks: to come alongside the hurting, and in turn teach them to do the same. Who better to train up to release in to the community that guys and girls who understand the pain, but also truly know the hope there is in Jesus?

I am a firm believer in family and community. It is the home of transformation. It is the place where 'decisions' for Jesus will become sold-out disciples for him. Families are the places where we learn to love and be loved, where we learn to dream and feel safe enough to pursue those dreams without fear of failure or want of compromise. We are wired for connection and in an atmosphere of love people flourish. We simply learn to be. There is a beautiful paraphrase of Ephesians 4:15 in the Mirror Bible: 'Love gives truth a voice and creates an atmosphere wherein growth is both spontaneous and inevitable.' I truly believe The Oaks is a place where those previously branded the 'burdens' of society will become the nation's blessings as they learn to truly live with Jesus and for Jesus. I feel incredibly privileged that I get to play a part in their stories.

The Oaks officially opened its doors this summer after our MEC Building Team did a wonderful job of renovating an abandoned shell of a house into a large family home.

This is a beautiful picture of what we dream of seeing in countless lives. At the time of writing we have our first five residents, all referrals from our prisons team and rehab centres, and a few more likely to be with us in the next few months. They come in to a structured programme of discipleship, but more than that, they come in to community. We get to live the gospel with them, rather than simply teach it to them.

As I write this, I can hear the sound of laughter emanating from the kitchen as the guys cook tea together. I know their stories. I know that for them, this is far from normal. A few weeks ago, Joe was teaching me how to cook rice, and as he did so shared some of his story with me – his first memory being of his six-year-old brother Tommy, being rushed to hospital to have his stomach pumped after drinking a bottle of his alcoholic parents' cider; his last memory of his mum was watching her being put into the back of an ambulance after suffering a stroke whilst at the same time rummaging through her purse for drugs money. He told me about watching his brother die of a heroin overdose in front of his eyes, finding another young guy dead in his accommodation, not to mention countless years in and out of jail in between. The list goes on and on. Stories that would shatter the heart of most, for Joe have been his 'normal'. Three months in, Joe's 'normal' is changing – so much so that this week he offered to accompany Bridget, our 70-year-old cook, to ballroom dancing lessons! When we're loved, we start to love. Similarly, with Ste, his greatest hope is to be a good husband and dad. Family is not something he has ever had modelled well in his life. In The Oaks he gets to learn as he watches Simon live his life, loving his wife and children close up.

We see their struggles, but we don't let our vision stop there. One of the first events we held at The Oaks was a 'Five Years Clean' party for one of our honorary family members and a great inspiration to the lads in the house, Laura. Celebrating freedom with a BBQ, a water fight and copious amounts of cake, the house was filled with laughter. And in celebrating the one, I dreamed for the many. I want to be at all our guys' 'Five Years Clean' parties someday. But our dream is for them to be more than just clean. We dream about being at their weddings, their kids' birthdays, their graduations, their churches.... We dream of them living in the fullness of the freedom that Jesus paid for them.

One of the simplest, yet most moving, prayers I have ever heard was from another one of our guys, Gary. Just a week in to his being with us I was taking communion with him, Ste and Joe. His prayer: 'Jesus, thank you for family.' And as I stood with them looking at the bread and wine I knew more than ever that this – this Christ-centred love, connection and community – is the true home of transformation. Ephesians 2 tells us that, 'Because of and in order to satisfy the great and wonderful and intense love with which He loved us...' he sent his son to die. I think The Oaks goes some way in presenting that acceptance, that belonging and that love of Christ to these guys.

It's for that reason that I don't intend to call The Oaks work. I intend to call it home.

THE RICHEST WORD IN THE BIBLE

CHAPTER SEVEN

ISAIAH 54:10

'Though the mountains be shaken

    and the hills be removed,

yet my unfailing love for you will not be shaken

    nor my covenant of peace be removed,'

    says the Lord, who has compassion on you.

Isaiah 54:10

It's about peace with God. Who can touch a man or woman for whom that truly is their experience?

What's the richest word in The Bible? Here's what I think it is: it's *shalom*. *Shalom* is better than peace, it's peace that passes understanding. It's peace that the world can't give. It's something so indescribably beautiful that with it we are unbelievably rich, without it we're unbelievably poor. It's the peace of God that's ours because he was 'crushed for our iniquities'.

It's something that the world without Jesus can never know. No amount of fame, no amount of success, no amount of worldly pleasure can bring this kind of peace. Look at the people who in the world's eyes have got it all. They're chaos! Do you know why? Because they're chasing after a peace that this world brings, and yet it never does.

Shalom is an amazing gospel word: it means centredness, contentment, complete wholeness and wellbeing. That's what we're meant to be walking in, through thick and thin. It's the full enjoyment of God. *Shalom* is about being in right relationship. It's about peace with God. Who can touch a man or woman for whom that truly is their experience? And it should be our experience because of the cross. We can receive the incredible *shalom* of God. One day we're going to experience the full measure of it and what a beautiful day that will be. But actually, today, we're supposed to experience a fair share of it – and I think we're meant to experience it in increasing measure.

The floodgates are open

Isaiah 54 comes (surprise, surprise) after Isaiah 53, and it's like the floodgates of God's blessing are now open. It's like a river flowing out of the cross and the resurrection, a beautiful picture of a people made right with God – all the curses, all the rejection, all the wrath is gone and suddenly we're in this perfect relationship with God.

Listen to verse 10: *'My unfailing love for you will not be shaken nor my covenant of peace be removed," says the Lord, who has compassion on you.'*

Drink these words in – they're for you. But they're not just for you – they're for your kids, too. Here's verse 13: '*All your children will be taught by the Lord, and great will be their peace.*' Great will be their *shalom*! It's great for us to stand under the blessing of God in the here and now but it's for the generations to come. And not just physical kids, but *spiritual* kids, too.

What about this where it says 'the Lord is your husband?' We often think of the Lord as our father, don't we? And if we can get really intimate, we think of the Lord as our friend: Jesus said 'I'm no longer calling you servants, I'm calling you friends' (John 15:15). That's an amazing thing in itself. But here Isaiah says twice that the Lord is our *husband*. Now, that can feel a bit weird as a man, but actually what the Lord is saying is that this is the most intimate relationship, the closest relationship possible, where everything is shared, where everything is laid bare, that's the relationship he wants to have with us.

Do you ever walk out on a starry night and think 'wow'? When I was in South Africa recently we stayed in this really isolated place, and at night there's no light pollution whatsoever. You go outside and it's truly breathtaking. Well, that's just a tiny, tiny bit of God's creation, this vast, vast universe. He's the one that's saying, 'I'm your husband. I want to come that close to you. I want to be that intimate, and pour my love on you'. The best husbands have love and respect, but also deep compassion towards their wives. And this is our Lord, a perfect picture of a compassionate husband.

Made for *shalom*

The Lord says, 'With deep compassion I will bring you back' (verse 7) and that resonates with our message of a gospel of repentance and forgiveness. It's not God's heart that young people in Manchester die and are separate from God. It's not his heart. He who went through the cross – our husband, the Lord, the one who's so close to us, the one who has deep compassion, the one who died for us and is alive again.

I love the way Ezekiel speaks of this in Ezekiel 18:32 – '*I take no pleasure in the death of anyone, declares the Sovereign Lord. Repent and live*'. That's our message with Higher, with Eden, with all our work with young people. The Lord wants no one to die, he wants no one to be lost. The Lord's heart is to save everyone, he died for everyone. Even stronger than that, read Ezekiel 33, verse 11 – '*Say to them, "As surely as I live, declares the Sovereign Lord, I take no pleasure in the death of the wicked, but rather that they turn from their ways and live. Turn!"*' That's us, isn't it? That's our message.

That was the baton that was passed on at the Great Commission. God doesn't want anyone to die and go to hell, he wants everyone to be saved.

He says, 'Go to them and tell them they can know the peace of God. They can know the *shalom* of God. This is our compassionate, gracious, kind God who will go to any lengths to see that we don't get what we deserve.

God chooses us! He says come close, become intimate, get centred, get real, live right, enjoy all the benefits of being a child of God. How rich we are! Yet so often we just go through our lives snuffling around, thinking small and living small when actually I've got so much in Jesus. So let's repent! Let's live in the *shalom* of God, not just now but forever. The full measure is what we're offering people – that's what we're inviting people to when we say come and join us.

REFLECTION

1. What does the *shalom* of God mean to you? To what extent are you living in it?

2. 'With deep compassion I will bring you back' (7). Try to identify any things which may be keeping you from the full *shalom* of God, repent and be forgiven of them.

3. Please pray with us that we'll see more opportunities to 'put the lamp on a stand' in every corner around the nation.

PRAYER

It's all about you, Jesus. Thank you that you're big enough to save every person. Thank you for the cross, that you went through that for us. Lord, everyone must know and understand of your great love, that you did what was necessary.

Amen

'I'm just so grateful that I'm not just another statistic or another offender'

Andy adds: Ruth Devent works full-time in our Mess Café at the Message Enterprise Centre (MEC). She first came to work with us while still serving a prison sentence. Following a very dark time in her life one of our prisons teams played a key part in Ruth's journey of transformation. From a broken life of violent abuse and addictions now God has completely restored her.

I was brought up in Moss Side, Manchester in quite a dysfunctional family. My parents split up when we were very young and for many years I was physically abused by my mum, who was an alcoholic.

When I reached my early teens I turned to hard core raving at the Hacienda in Manchester to escape from all of the pain. I then went from being addicted to ecstasy to alcohol.

Later when I was married with three children the drink still had a hold on me and I lost my husband and my kids.

I did get my life back on track for a while when I graduated from Manchester University with a degree in criminology in 2008. But after having another child my life went out of control again.

I ended up in an alcohol dependent relationship, which led to me going to HM Prison Styal for a wounding offence. So I was really in a dark place. I was very angry, confused and lost.

But all that began to change on the first morning when I met the prison chaplain. I asked her if she could pray for the victim of my offence and his family as well as my own my family which she did.

Then she offered me a New Testament which I took upstairs to my room. The first scripture I turned to was from Matthew 11 – 'Come to me all who are weary...' and I thought, 'That's me.' I then had an argument with God saying 'if you're real prove it because I want to rest, I'm tired of this.' That night I repented and said sorry for everything I'd done and asked God to forgive me if he loved me and I went to sleep.

The next morning, I felt really calm and when I spoke to the chaplain she asked me if I gave my life to Jesus. I said I hadn't technically but she said I actually had and she encouraged me to continue to read my New Testament.

After that I kept going to chapel wanting to know so much more, which is how I met Natalie Stanton, who was part of the Message prisons team and I joined their Bible study group. I had so many questions about how to have this peace and freedom. Natalie broke it down for me.

It was unbelievable because for the first eight weeks I was in a single cell and I absolutely devoured the New Testament. I stopped swearing and smoking. My whole attitude just changed. It was unbelievable because I was so angry when I first got there. I was growling at everyone. I wasn't a very nice person. I was always on the defensive,

very judgemental and just wanted to lock myself away from everybody.

But now I didn't want to be seen as this violent, angry woman. There was a lot of hurt there and fear. I realised I could give it all to God and I thought, this is amazing, I am actually loved. It just completely changed me. I'd been completely broken and now God was rebuilding me. I knew this was part of his plan for me because there was no other way he could've gotten through to me.

Officers noticed such a change in me they moved me to an open unit in the prison. Then they asked me if I would like to work at the Message Enterprise Centre. I knew Natalie worked there and she explained to me it was a café and they do a lot of work with ex-offenders and I was flabbergasted. For someone to put their trust in me gave me such a sense of hope.

When I was released from prison I was amazed when I was offered a full-time job at the MEC. I'm still in shock really. There are people working here who are going through what I've been through and I have been able to support them and tell them that they need to pray and ask God for help.

My life wouldn't be where it is now if it wasn't for The Message Trust. It's not just a job that they've given me. They've given me self-worth and I feel so valued as a team member. I'm just so grateful that they've given me this opportunity to show that I'm not just another statistic or another offender. I've made some wonderful life-long friendships. This is the best foundation for me to build on.

God has now restored my family life back to even better than it's ever been. I'm actually back with my husband now after he saw such a change in me. My daughter is stunned that she's got a mum. When I left she was 8. She's 18 now and I've got a really good relationship with her and she trusts me again. This is God and I thank him every day.

TWIN TRACKS OF MISSION

CHAPTER EIGHT

ISAIAH 55:6-13

Seek the Lord while he may be found;

    call on him while he is near.

Let the wicked forsake their ways

    and the unrighteous their thoughts.

Let them turn to the Lord, and he will have mercy on them,

    and to our God, for he will freely pardon.

"For my thoughts are not your thoughts,

    neither are your ways my ways,"

declares the Lord.

"As the heavens are higher than the earth,

    so are my ways higher than your ways

    and my thoughts than your thoughts.

As the rain and the snow come down from heaven,

and do not return to it without watering the earth

and making it bud and flourish,

    so that it yields seed for the sower and bread for the eater,

so is my word that goes out from my mouth:

    It will not return to me empty,

but will accomplish what I desire

and achieve the purpose for which I sent it.

You will go out in joy and be led forth in peace;

the mountains and hills will burst into song before you,

and all the trees of the field will clap their hands.

Instead of the thornbush will grow the juniper,

and instead of briers the myrtle will grow.

This will be for the Lord's renown,

for an everlasting sign,

that will endure forever."

Isaiah 55:6-13

The key is expectant faith

I often say that The Message locomotive runs on twin tracks of prayer and mission. I have a pair of framed scissors in my office that someone sent to me after a talk I gave once. On one blade it says 'Keep prayer hot' on the other it says 'Keep mission hot', and underneath it says 'Keep on the cutting edge, Andy'. That's it: the cutting edge for The Message is hot prayer and hot mission. And we need both, all the time. One without the other won't work. Prayer on its own can become *pious* – it becomes all about 'us' and our spiritual experiences and our spiritual welfare. And mission on its own can become *powerless*.

But these aren't the only 'perfect partners' in the life of The Message. There are others, too. There's **word** and **deed**: we're people who don't just preach, but we demonstrate the gospel. Again, one without the other doesn't work. If we're all 'deed' we're basically just social workers. And if we're all 'word', we're just mouthy people who've got a message but don't earth it, don't root it in demonstrating the love of Christ. So we never see the real transformation that comes through both word and deed.

Here's another perfect partner for The Message: Word and Spirit. We're people who are passionately committed to the Word of God and more than anything what I long to see is a movement of Bible-teaching evangelists. People who believe in the authority of the word of God and who actually teach it. But they must be empowered by the Holy Spirit. As someone said: 'Word only, you dry up. Spirit only, you blow up. Word and Spirit is the way we grow up.'

Isaiah 55 gives us two more perfect partners, another set of tracks that get the great big powerful Message locomotive moving faster as we step up our international work, grow the Eden Network and our prison stuff, as we roll out more and more buses, as we bring the Higher Tour to more and more places. The two things that I want to see modelled at The Message, that I want to live with day by day, are excitement and urgency.

Excitement

We need to be a bit more excited about this faith of ours. Isaiah 55 throbs with excitement and passion, it's buzzing with expectant faith. My old rector always used to say 'The key is expectant faith'. What a challenge! Are you living with expectant faith? Because without that we're not going to see all we want to see. Faith that God's about to change everything, and in Isaiah 55 of course, everything has changed because of the death of this suffering servant. You know there's all this doom and gloom across the nation and there's people living in captivity, but Isaiah speaks a better word and then he explains the full measure of the salvation that's going to come one day to the suffering servant. The word of the Lord changes everything.

Back in 1987, Manchester, in lots of ways, was a pretty barren place spiritually. The Bishop of Manchester at the time said he wasn't aware of a single lively youth group in the whole of Manchester Diocese – not one in 364 churches he oversaw. The city's church leaders were well known for falling out with one another. Youth were haemorrhaging from the church faster probably than in any place on Earth.

But then the Lord speaks to us about rivers in the desert, streams in the wasteland, wild animals honouring him. God speaks to the city, to a dry place – and suddenly passion comes, excitement comes. It happened again,

I believe, for me, as God spoke through Isaiah 60 and said the least will become a thousand, the smallest a mighty nation. 'Arise, shine, for your light has come'.

We have expectant faith because we've had the word of the Lord. Even through the difficult stuff – the challenges of working with people, the challenges of finances, the challenge of waiting on God's timing, of sickness and unanswered prayer – even through it all, we can remain passionate and excited. People who are excited about their faith are attractive people. I want to surround myself with people where I'm having to say, 'Will you just calm down a bit?'. Wouldn't it be great going around churches in the UK going 'Will you lot just be a little less enthusiastic? Just stop getting so excited, will you, about God?' George Verwer said 'It's easier to cool down a furnace than warm up a corpse'. That's what we should be! A furnace of the Holy Spirit, on fire for God!

Urgency

The other track is urgency. Because you see, there's a banquet that everyone's invited to, but you must accept the invitation. '*Come, all you who are thirsty, come to the waters; and you who have no money, come, buy and eat! Come, buy wine and milk without money and without cost*' (verse 1).

My wife Michelle loves to host – she is the hostess with the mostess – and she's a brilliant cook. So we invite lots of people to eat with us at home. What really gets on my nerves is when someone phones up an hour before they're due to arrive to say, 'Oh, sorry, I can't come'. Have you ever had that? When we've gone to a load of trouble getting ready for them it feels like they're saying, 'Oh, I've got a better offer'.

But that's nothing compared to when we pass on God's invitation. After all the effort that God's gone to – sending his own son to Earth, bankrupting heaven, Jesus dying on that cross taking the full wrath of God for sin. Think of all that's gone through and now he says come, come to the banquet, come to heaven because of this let heaven invade you, let the holy spirit invade you. Come. But we do it all the time. We pass up the great invitation of God to come. And often, we just say, 'Oh, I can't be bothered, I've got a better offer'.

There needs to be an urgency alongside our excitement about our salvation. Forgiveness is available, but time is running out. '*Seek the Lord while he may be found, call on him while he is near. Let the wicked forsake their ways and the unrighteous their thoughts. Let them turn to the Lord and he will have mercy on them, and to our God, for he will freely pardon*' (verse 7).

The evangelist's urgency

Listen to Reinhard Bonnke: 'The gospel is eternal, but we haven't eternity to preach it. One would think we had that long when we view the often leisurely operations of the church on the gospel front. We have only as long as we live to reach those who live as long as we live. Today over seven billion souls are alive in our present world. Not in some indefinite future age which needs to be evangelised, this is the last hour.'

Can you hear the evangelist's urgency? He goes on: 'Many churches are very active, but active doing what? Fiddling about with secular issues is one way to look impressively busy and relevant but to bring the gospel to a dying world is true relevance. Giving all our thoughts to our personal spirituality when the fires of hell have broken out is like members of the fire brigade having a shave before answering a fire call. We can spend years standing for our principles when we're only justifying our church quarrels and prejudices. The command to evangelise is all that matters'.

I once heard David Watson say 'Compared to evangelism, everything else that's happening in the church is like rearranging the furniture while the house is on fire'. And he's right. Our mission as The Message is to be people who are like salt in the church, flavouring it with a passion for evangelism. We're excited about this gospel, we're excited about evangelism and we're urgent about it. We're people who've got to do crazy things because it's urgent, because young people are dying without Christ. All the evidence is if you don't get young people by the time they're 20, you don't get them at all. According to the statistics, the average age of conversion is 14, and if you don't get people by the time they're 20 their hearts become hard and calloused to the things of God. So let's have a fresh measure of urgency alongside our excitement.

REFLECTION

1. Are you living with expectant faith? Do you need more expectancy of God at work in your life? In your family? In your church?

2. Make a list of the things you are most excited about in life and then put them in order of urgency.

3. Are you letting any lesser things get in the way of the most important thing – the mission of God?

PRAYER

Lord, make us a church that is both excited and urgent about our mission. Take us to new places on these twin tracks and please give us more opportunities to reach hundreds of thousands for you.

Amen

TESTIMONY:
EMMA WILKINSON

'God's faithfulness has been the cornerstone of the past seven years'

Andy adds: Emma is a former Urban Hero Award winner and one of the most outstanding young people we've ever worked with. Her story shows what God can do with a young life when they choose to follow him and say, 'Here I am, send me!' It's also a great example of why we need many more Eden teams reaching out to young people in local communities.

Friday 4 September 2009 was my first day at secondary school. The closest school to our house was on the Buttershaw council estate, so it was the obvious choice for both my brother and me who were in the same school year. As we walked to 'big school' that morning our doting parents took photos of us at every pretty wall and garden fence. In fact, they took so many photos that we were late for our first day! As we ran into the school building a teacher shouted at us that this wasn't a very good start to our time in secondary school.

Looking back now though, that teacher was so wrong: I had the best possible start. That week the school newsletter had an advert for the school's Christian Union that had just been set up by the local church, Buttershaw Baptist. I went along and within a month I was so struck by God's love for me that I made the decision to follow Jesus.

It wasn't long after this that Gavin Humphries, the Eden Buttershaw team leader, and his wife Maz moved onto Buttershaw. They quickly invited me to Buttershaw Baptist, the church the Eden team had partnered with. Maz drew me a map on a scrap of orange paper and on the first Sunday in February 2010 my Mum came with me to the afternoon family service. As soon as we walked through the door we were loved as if we were family and so we went back the next week, and the week after that. Soon, Maz invited my Mum over for lunch, explained the gospel to her and gave her a copy of 'Why Jesus?'. One early morning that spring, my Mum read that tract and made the decision to follow Jesus alone in our living room.

Around this time, I made the decision to be baptised, so my Dad came along to a Sunday service at church to see 'what I was getting myself into.' In the middle of the sermon, I turned around to see him crying, having been hit by the power of the Holy Spirit. Our amazing minister climbed over chairs to reach my Dad and pray with him. It was right then, right there, that my Dad gave his life to Jesus. When I reflect on how each of us started our journey with God, I'm taken aback with how different those experiences were, yet it makes complete sense. God, who knows and loves us personally, met each of us exactly where we were.

Over that following summer, God spoke to us as a family. Buttershaw was the council estate my Dad grew up on in the late 1970s although it was built 20 years earlier. The decline of traditional industries in the 1980s saw unemployment, crime and drug use rise exponentially, all of which are still issues today, along with low educational achievement and other signs of deprivation. That's why the area was chosen for an Eden team – and why Gav and Maz had moved in. We felt God calling us to join them there by moving onto the estate.

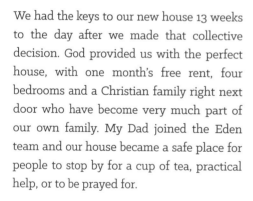

Emma with the Urban Hero Inspiration Award 2012

We had the keys to our new house 13 weeks to the day after we made that collective decision. God provided us with the perfect house, with one month's free rent, four bedrooms and a Christian family right next door who have become very much part of our own family. My Dad joined the Eden team and our house became a safe place for people to stop by for a cup of tea, practical help, or to be prayed for.

As I headed back to school that autumn, I prayed a dangerous prayer: 'God, use me.' By the end of Year 9, I was leading the Christian Union and had set up a Peer Pastoral Team in school. I began doing assemblies and teaching RE lessons, even teaching GCSE RE to my own class when our teacher was on maternity leave. I quickly became known around school as 'Christian Emma', a nickname that provided many opportunities to chat to people and to pray for them. Before I knew it, I was praying for teachers

too and seeing God heal people in the classroom. When I asked God to use me, he took me seriously.

But the opportunities God provided me with to serve in school were met by relentless bullying. The nickname of 'Christian Emma' soon became used as an insult as I was sworn at, spat at, threatened and even had stones thrown at me. I often joke that it is a miracle I was only ever physically assaulted once in those seven years. Friendships became difficult to maintain as being associated with me around school didn't make people very popular, especially as the bullying I endured was sometimes encouraged by teachers. Break times and lunch times became a nightmare so I often spent them in the RE department, talking to the teachers there, and while that didn't help with people liking me, I learnt so much from them. The RE department became a place of sanctuary for me, I could go there and pray or talk nonsense and feel valued within school.

Then a strange thing happened: as I continued to ask God to use me, those who were the most vicious in bullying me became the ones who would find me after class to ask me to pray for them. In this season I learnt what it really means to have Jesus as both my Lord and my friend, but I still consistently prayed for a genuine friendship. Our faithful God provided a truly faithful friend who is now my best friend: the daughter of my minister. We have a similar heart for serving God, a passion for the good news of Jesus and series of inside jokes no one else can understand. Her encouragement and friendship is invaluable to me and as I continue to learn from her, I'm reminded of how she is a testimony to God's faithfulness.

In Year 11, just after my 16th birthday, the Eden team put on a schools week in my secondary school, and I had the honour of helping to lead it. It was a week of RE lessons, after-school activities and a gig on the Friday night with Vital Signs. That final evening 81 young people responded to the good news of Jesus and, standing in the room as they received prayer, I was overwhelmed by the goodness of God. This was what I had been praying for – for five years. God, being steadfast, had turned up and changed lives.

I went to the Sixth Form attached to the secondary school and continued to serve Jesus the best I could. My locker became full of spare pens and bottles of water that people could get whenever they needed to. I talked about Jesus in the common room and in the classroom and found that the

bullying was no longer vicious as my peers realised that there was no way to stop me from sharing Jesus with those around me. In the final year of my A Levels I became ill, and that meant that from January was too ill to go to school. Instead I studied at home and sat my exams in a spare room at home that June. In those six months I was also told that I wouldn't be well enough to go to university that autumn. I felt as if my plan for my life was being derailed, but still God is faithful. When I met with Gavin, I asked whether in this forced year out I could help out with 'some Eden stuff' and by the end of the conversation he commented that I might as well do an internship. Out of the ruins of my plan, God fashioned an internship with Eden Buttershaw, a brilliant opportunity to serve God that I wasn't expecting. No matter how good I think God is, he is always better. Despite being ill when I sat my A Level exams I came out with results of A* A* A by God's grace alone.

In my journey with God so far, I've fallen in love with the church, believing it is the hope of the world, and convinced in the importance of incarnational ministry like that of Eden. God's faithfulness has been the cornerstone of the past seven years and I suppose that from time to time, I still think about that 11-year-old girl who was late on her first day of secondary school, unaware of the adventure that it would be. Writing this at the end of that era and the beginning of a new one challenges me to continue to ask God to use me. After all, I had the best start to secondary school when I was given the opportunity to follow Jesus because the the Eden team on Buttershaw and the local church together were willing to pray the dangerous prayer of 'God, use me'.

SIN KILLS

CHAPTER NINE

But your iniquities have separated you from your God;

your sins have hidden his face from you, so that he will not hear.

For your hands are stained with blood,

    your fingers with guilt.

Your lips have spoken falsely,

    and your tongue mutters wicked things.

He put on righteousness as his breastplate,

    and the helmet of salvation on his head;

he put on the garments of vengeance

    and wrapped himself in zeal as in a cloak.

"The Redeemer will come to Zion,

    to those in Jacob who repent of their sins,"

declares the Lord.

Isaiah 59:2-3, 17, 20

"

True repentance has been at the heart of every major move of God

Christians tend to go to one of two extremes when they talk about sin. They can be all about the rules and regulations, like 'Don't smoke, don't drink, don't dance, don't go to the sin-ema!' Or much more likely in this generation, they can go to the opposite extreme of licence, lax about sex, drink or whatever it is. Often we don't talk about sin enough. But we should – because the Bible does, a lot.

I first got serious about God aged 17. I'd made a sort of commitment when I was 12 but I didn't live like it mattered and I became a rebel at school. In fact I was told by the headmaster that I was the worst pupil that had ever been to the school (I was quite proud of that really). So when the RE teacher heard that Andy Hawthorne, the worst pupil, the nightmare kid, had become a Christian – and not just a Christian but a raving evangelist who was going round all the pubs in Cheadle witnessing and trying to lead his mates to Jesus left, right and centre – he phoned me up. 'Would you come in and take a day of RE lessons?' he asked.

At this point, I'd only been a full-on Christian for a few weeks so I was a bit taken aback. But I said OK, and next thing I know I was being wheeled into school for back-to-back lessons where I was standing there giving my testimony for an hour at a time. Trying to make it a little more engaging, I brought along a boom box with a cassette of an Irish Christian punk band (I can't even remember what they're called now) with a song that went 'I wanna hate it, hate it, sin kills!' It was great. After three minutes of loud punk, I said, 'Actually, I believe that. I believe sin kills, it destroys, it will destroy you, it separates you from Christ. But you can be forgiven for your sins today.'

In a way, 40 years on, nothing much has changed and Isaiah 59 reminds us why.

True repentance

Let's be honest: true repentance, repentance that is the doorway into the blessed life, doesn't come easily to us. We're naturally self-centred people.

We're going our way and if God's way is the opposite way, we don't want to turn around and truly repent. Isaiah 59 verses 2 and 3 remind us, '*Your iniquities have separated you from your God; your sins have hidden his face from you, so that he will not hear. For your hands are stained with blood, your fingers with guilt.*'

You really notice it when very sinful people get saved. People who've lived dark lives very often show it on their faces. And when these people who were deeply into depravity and addiction and all kinds of criminality meet Jesus their whole countenance changes. I've seen it happen in moments. One of my friends became a Christian backstage at Spring Harvest and she'd been a goth, she was into drug culture, pretty wild sexual depravity and all sorts of craziness, and honestly my chin hit the floor when she said, 'Andy I've given my life to Jesus tonight.' As I'm looking at her, suddenly I see a new beauty coming through.

The stain of sin screws everything up – that's why we should hate it. We've got to hate it in our own lives and our own hearts, we've got to hate its destructive effects on our world and we've got to hate the fact that my sin nailed my saviour to the cross. It wasn't the nails that held him there, it was my sin. He had to go through that because I'm such a wicked sinner.

True repentance has been at the heart of every major move of God. And we believe God has promised us much more than we've seen thus far at The Message. We believe he's promised us a major move of God amongst young people in our lifetime. He's promised us rivers in the desert, the righteousness of this cause will shine like the noonday sun. And a sure sign will be repentance.

Revival built on repentance

Perhaps you know that William Booth and the early days of the Salvation Army have been our great inspiration as a movement. It was an incredible move of God among the least, the last and the lost. They saw hundreds of thousands swept into the kingdom through bold proclamation, incredible sacrifice and unbelievable adventures on behalf of the poor – orphanages, schools, hostels and just amazing stuff, all in the power of the Spirit.

If you're wondering what people of the day made of it, here's a description of a Salvation Army meeting from 1879, written by a cynical journalist in the Newcastle Daily Chronicle: "The sweep of dancing and shouting and glory to God could be heard everywhere, and yet as may be seen and as I've written, until penitents throw themselves at the feet of Jesus as it's called, a meeting of the Salvation Army is a tolerably sane affair. The fat is at once in the fire, however when penitents come forward... half a dozen crop-headed youths, boys they are, are praying vociferously with their faces towards me. Did I say praying? I only suppose it were praying, they were shouting with closed eyes, the bodies were swaying to and fro, the hands were lifted and they were brought down again with a thump on the form, they contorted themselves as if they were in acute agony'.

He goes on to say, '...meanwhile the hallelujah lasses were busy about the work of conversion.' The hallelujah lasses were William Booth's ministry team. They were all ex-junkies, street women and prostitutes, and they would minister to people as they came forward as 'penitents', in other words, those who repent of their sins and receive forgiveness from God. God, give us more penitents in schools! God, give us some penitents in prison! God, give us an army of penitents; people who truly repent of their sins and receive real forgiveness! This is how he ends his article: 'When I reached the street after the meeting in the pure air, it was fresh grey morning, the meeting had gone on all night. "Is this a common sort of thing here?", I asked the policeman outside. "Very", he said, "But it's certainly reduced our charge sheet. I haven't had a case to try in two months"'.

That's revival – built on repentance and conviction of sin. Built on radical prayer – their prayer meetings went on all night. Built on amazing sacrifice, lots of them died and the churches were trashed in this period, but crime stopped, and thousands were swept into the kingdom. God give us the real thing! God give us penitents.

The Lord, the warrior

We have this amazing picture in Isaiah 59 of our God responding to our plight, and rising up as a warrior on his almighty rescue battle to rescue us from our sins. Look at verse 17: 'He put on righteousness as his breastplate and the helmet of salvation on his head'. This is a picture of our God coming against our sin. He wrapped himself in zeal as a cloak and put on the armaments of vengeance. Can you see the picture of love and justice in perfect partnership? God's salvation and righteousness poured down on a needy people, but also his zeal, his vengeance, his wrath against sin. Let's stop presenting our God as this lovey-dovey, wishy-washy life coach whose job it is to give us a great life and who could never punish sin, because it's all about us. This is not the God of the Bible.

Finally verse 20 sums it up perfectly. It sums up the whole book, I think: *'The redeemer will come to Zion, for those in Jacob who repent of their sins declared the Lord.'* In the light of all this fearful talk of the terrifying effects of sin there's a way out. There's a way for the stain to be removed and for us to be made right, for us to be pure and holy. The barrier's removed, the separation is removed and it comes through a redeemer. And sure enough, 600 years after these words were written by Isaiah, the Redeemer came and his message was 'the kingdom of Heaven is near. Repent and believe the good news'. And everywhere Jesus went he left penitents.

Jesus preached repentance and he did it because he hated sin with every fibre of his being. Why did he weep when he looked on Jerusalem? Because he saw the destructive effects of sin on his people and he just longed to gather them up, for them to be forgiven and free, and he did everything that was necessary for that to happen.

Look at the beauty of people who pursue righteousness and holiness, and don't allow sin to tangle them. Yes, they sin, but they quickly repent, they walk in repentance. They get time with the Lord every day to allow the illuminating Holy Spirit to reveal to them what's wrong and what offends him, because they hate sin. They do it because they want to be at the cutting edge of God's purposes. What they want to know is the full wholeness of the Holy Spirit, but the Holy Spirit only fully fills holy people.

That's what the Message is about. We're not about running a charity; we're about rescuing people from hell. We're about removing the destructive, deadly force of sin in this generation and the only way it can be removed is through the blood of Jesus.

REFLECTION

1. What's your faith story? At what point did you finally repent of your sins and accept forgiveness?

2. How do you feel about boldly calling people to repentance?

3. 'The Holy Spirit only fully fills holy people.' Ask God to show you areas in your life in which you can become more holy, in order to be more fully filled.

PRAYER

Lord, help us to look for revival every day as we boldly call people to repentance of sin. May we see many ugly, broken lives be made beautiful and fully restored in our generation.

Amen

INTO THE WILD
SAM WARD

Sam is our National Director for the Eden Network, responsible for rolling out community-changing Edens in the nation's toughest neighbourhoods.

When I think about 'the wild' I think about extreme adventure. I imagine an intrepid explorer, machete in hand, slashing at untouched vegetation. There is something deeply appealing about adventure – the balance of risk and exploration and having your courage, endurance and skill tested to its limits.

Although born and raised in the wilds of rural Shropshire, I now consider myself a city boy. My jungle is concrete these days; I've lived in Manchester for well over 20 years and the closest I get to wild vegetation is mowing the small plot of grass I call my garden.

But on the odd occasion that I walk visitors around my community it's clear that they consider my neighbourhood to be wild. In the past people have commented as to whether their cars are safe and if their belongings are best left inside my house before I take them on the safari tour. All this

feels so odd. It's very rare that I experience any kind of fear whilst living here. Living on an estate in the inner city is far from wild for me. That doesn't make me some kind of hero. I'm by no means a hard man. I've simply made this community my home. After 15 years this place is familiar. People aren't faces; they're friends.

I do, however, regularly attempt to venture into the wild. Not the odd day out in the peak district or a scramble up a Pennine rock face. I mean wild on far more dangerous level: the extreme adventure of deep living, of genuine relationships. I aspire to be Bear Grylls-esque in my pursuit of sincere affection and fearless friendship. I long to love on a deeper level; learning to understand others in a profoundly rich yet wild way.

These depths are not easily plumbed; you have to push on hard through superficiality and take a machete to layer after layer of self-preservation and pretence to reach the

often-obscured path of real relationship. I find the journey seriously tiring. It's hard going, risky and extremely costly at times. But it is also the way you can discover amazing new places.

The following stories from two recent Message Trust Urban Hero Awards winners give an insight into some of the places that can be found when Eden teams embark upon these journeys to see the lives God is working in.

SARAH

Customers at the Mess Café at the Message Enterprise Centre in Wythenshawe are usually greeted by Sarah, a confident young woman with a big smile and a sunny disposition. Among the few people who know how far she's come is Lizzie, a team member on Eden Openshaw in Manchester.

'We first met Sarah when she started coming to a lunchtime club that the Eden team was putting on for more vulnerable Year 7 pupils in our local high school. Sarah was really shy; we used to call her little Sarah,' shares Lizzie.

Sarah describes how she wouldn't go out or talk to anyone. Staying at home all the time

she didn't like mixing with other people. 'They'd take the mick out of me. Just make me feel not wanted.'

The reason for Sarah's shyness included moderate learning difficulties and a strained home life. The Eden Openshaw team gave Sarah the support and sense of belonging she needed.

'I guess Sarah found a place where she felt safe and she was able to be herself,' reflects Lizzie. 'We were able to take her along to weekends away and camping and loads of fun new experiences she would probably not have had without Eden.'

As she began to put her trust in Christ, Sarah also found a confidence in herself and the Eden team was with her every step of the way.

'It made a big difference because I was able to open up and actually speak to Lizzie about my problems because I wasn't able to speak to my mum because of the way she was. I'd be able to talk to Lizzie, meet up with her, read the Bible, pray together, just do stuff I probably wouldn't do in front of lots of people.'

Once she left school it became clear that finding a job was going to be a real challenge. She offered to volunteer at the Message Enterprise Centre. Her attitude and determination impressed the team so much that the café offered her a full time job working alongside the message team and ex-offenders and her confidence went through the roof.

'I've come out of my shell. I'm more focused on Jesus as well and not other things. Nothing else bothers me; it's all in the past now.'

For Lizzie, it's all been worth it: 'It's such a privilege to have seen Sarah as she's grown up and as she's got a job now in the Mess Café. She's just grown so much in confidence and she's just so proud of herself; her Mum and Dad are so proud of her and we're so proud of her.'

JAKE

Dreaming of being part of Everton Football Club, at the age of 16, football-mad Jake Mattocks thought he knew exactly how his life was going to turn out. Being born and raised in Netherton, a deprived part of Liverpool, he knew he wanted to do something to help his community too. So when he was signed up by the club as a trainee community coach it seemed like all his dreams had come true.

'I just want to be doing what they are doing, coaching in the community and helping people with difficulties in their lives.'

Everything seemed to be going brilliantly for Jake until out of nowhere he began to experience sudden uncontrollable blackouts.

'The NHS called them mental episodes where I would just blank out. I had no control of myself, didn't know what was going on at all until other people told me. I could have possibly killed myself jumping off a bridge but the police stopped me in time.'

Jake's life as he knew it came crashing down around him. He was placed under constant supervision unable to go out with groups or be around kids it meant his dream career coaching football was over.

'Everything just fell to pieces. I couldn't go out and see friends and just felt beaten up. Is this really what a boy my age should be going through? It felt like it was the end of my life.'

It was right then that an Eden team moved into the area and began talking to young people including Jake.

'I just felt like I could talk to them back. I just instantly clicked with Tom and Eden and the team individually. I got to know them and I felt part of a family.'

The Eden Netherton team brought Jake's faith alive and gave him opportunities to volunteer with youth clubs, mums and tots groups in church and more.

He's now a vital part of the team as an intern and hopes to join the team full time as a youth worker. Jake has not experienced a single blackout for 14 months.

'I love doing Eden work and I love being part of Eden. With youth clubs we're making good relationships with people and I know for a fact that God's going to save them. And I know he is because we're working as team.'

Eden Netherton's work is growing rapidly, in no small part because of Jake's natural ability to relate to kids on the estate.

'Without the work of Eden and the encouragement from Tom I wouldn't be able to just go up to random 17-year-old lads saying 'God loves you'. I just wouldn't be able to do that but now I could just go out there now and say 'God loves you, mate' without a problem.'

'He's a fantastic guy and it's been incredible to have him as part of the team and to see what God's doing in his life and how God's using him to transform the lives of other people in his community,' says Tom Grant, Eden Netherton's team leader.

Jake is now employed as an Eden Netherton Youth and Community Worker for three days a week and is back working at Everton Football Club doing community coaching another two days a week.

After seeing what happened in Jake's life, his mum Claire has also become a Christian and Jake and Tom baptised her together. She now volunteers at lots of Eden activities, sharing her faith with others.

COME WITH US

Living deeply comes with serious consequences. As we delve deeper we are confronted with a responsibility to radically care and comfort, to radically challenge and support. The truth is that relationship building is not an extreme sport that we do to others. As we begin the adventure into the wilds of true friendship, our first discovery is often that the thickest jungles are not found within the lives of those we attempt to serve or sort out but within our own lives. Living deep is mutually risky.

Since the first team launched back in 1997, over 400 people have taken on this risk, replicating our values across cities throughout the UK. We exist to recruit teams who will go on this journey in the poorest neighbourhoods – encouraging and equipping the people who join to see the gospel shared and disciples made.

As a Network we are on a journey of discovery, too. Our UK hubs in the North West, North East, Yorkshire and Humber, Midlands and London continue to expand. We are also breaking new ground in the UK, launching teams in Glasgow and Wales in recent years. In South Africa, three new teams are demonstrating that our approach can work worldwide in a completely different context. And will soon be going into new international territory as we launch our first team in Canada.

Whether people relocate to a new home, return to a community they once left or remain as lights in their current neighbourhoods, we are about calling more workers to the harvest. 'Join Eden' has become our bold recruitment call and we place this challenge front and centre to all as we move forward to see what God has in store next.

Let's take a machete called vulnerability and head on into the wild. Are you coming?

Find out more about Eden: **joineden.org**

GOOD
NEWS TO
THE POOR

CHAPTER TEN

ISAIAH 61:1-3

The Spirit of the Sovereign Lord is on me,

because the Lord has anointed me

to proclaim good news to the poor.

He has sent me to bind up the broken-hearted,

to proclaim freedom for the captives

and release from darkness for the prisoners,

to proclaim the year of the Lord's favour

and the day of vengeance of our God,

to comfort all who mourn,

and provide for those who grieve in Zion —

to bestow on them a crown of beauty

instead of ashes,

the oil of joy

instead of mourning,

and a garment of praise

instead of a spirit of despair.

They will be called oaks of righteousness,

a planting of the Lord

for the display of his splendour.

Isaiah 61:1-3

"

We need to wake up to just how high our calling is

I magine being Isaiah, anointed to prophesy about Jesus: 'This is the family he's going to be born into', 'This is what he's going to do with his life', 'This is where he's going to live', even 'This is where he's going to be born'... it's all prophesied by Isaiah under the anointing of the Holy Spirit. More than 300 very specific prophecies about the Messiah are all focused like a big spotlight on the Saviour. In the Bible there were one or two people who came and went and maybe fulfilled one or two of those prophecies. Maybe there were men who were born in Bethlehem who died on the cross, maybe there were people from David's family whose friends betrayed them, but there's only one man who fulfilled all 300-plus specific prophecies: Jesus Christ.

Isaiah says, 'The Spirit of the Sovereign Lord is on me and he's anointed me...' And when he says that, the people are meant to go 'Whoa! Okay, let's get ready for some revelation, let's get ready for something truly powerful now.' He says the Lord has anointed him for three things: To preach good news to the poor, to bind up the broken-hearted, to proclaim freedom for the captives and release from darkness for the prisoners. Later Jesus added, 'To open the eyes of the blind' to the list.

Down the centuries of the church there's been all sorts of arguments about what the focus of the church should be. Are we meant to open the eyes of the blind as a priority? Is it miracles that are meant to open the way to preach the gospel? Is it front-and-centre preaching of the word? Front and centre Bible preaching? Or is it that we're meant to pour our lives into the poor and the broken, and when they see our good deeds they'll praise our Father in heaven? Which is it? It's all of them, of course, because Jesus perfectly modelled all of them: words, works and wonders. What a beautiful rhythm Jesus modelled. And we see it clearly in Luke chapter 4 when it's Jesus' time to embark upon the incredible, world-changing, radical ministry Isaiah prophesied about.

Fulfilled in your hearing

I went to see U2 a little while ago and my mate bought me a ticket. It cost £184. I thought 'Wow, we're going to get some good food and good entertainment, and books signed by Bono, and I'm going to get to kiss The Edge's guitar or something... something good's got to happen for £184!' And all we got was access to a bar where we had to buy beer and a comfy seat with a padded cushion on. I mean, it was an amazing night, but perhaps not worth £184. But how much would you pay to have been in that synagogue that morning, listening to Jesus read the scriptures? *'The Spirit of the Sovereign Lord is on me and he has anointed me to preach good news to the poor, to bind up the broken-hearted, to open the eyes of the blind, to announce the year the Lord's favour'* (Luke 4:18-19).

Just something about the way he read those scriptures meant every eye was fastened on him, even before he sat down to preach his message. Normally a synagogue message would go on a bit, and normally it would be interactive. He would say something, people would ask questions, people would chip in and they'd debate things and discuss things. But not for Jesus. This was the most powerful, profound sermon the world's ever heard. It was firing the starting pistols of the great gospel rescue mission: *'Today this scripture is fulfilled in your hearing'* (21). Hundreds of years they'd been waiting since Isaiah spoke those words. And right now, these scriptures were being fulfilled. This is it.

And that's what he did for three-and-a-half years: preached good news to the poor, bound up the broken-hearted and opened the eyes of the blind. In Matthew 10, he invites a bunch of unschooled, ordinary, up-and-down, inconsistent guys to join in. He sent them out in his name and they started to do the stuff under the anointing of the Holy Spirit. Until it all seems to go wrong. After all the prophecies were fulfilled, after three-and-a-half years of incredible ministry, it all starts to go pear-shaped. Jesus gets arrested and tried and crucified. The disciples, even though they're unschooled and ordinary, they would have known their scriptures, that anyone who's nailed to a tree is cursed. That person can't be the Messiah. But look closely and you'll see that's all prophesied in the Old Testament too. It's even prophesied a thousand years before Christ – before crucifixions had even been invented – that he will be nailed, pierced through his hands and feet.

But they couldn't see it. They are just so blinded by their brokenness and their fear they had given up hope... until Jesus rises from the dead. He conquers sin and death, then spends time with them convincing them he really was the fulfilment of all the prophecies, he really was the Messiah. He makes breakfast for them on the beach, he teaches 500 of them in one place, he spends six weeks with them. Then he gathers them in John 21 and he says, 'Boys, it's time for me to go. I need to go now, back to my Father'. And the disciples respond, 'No way! You're not going anywhere, Jesus – you're not leaving us again.' But Jesus says, 'No, it's better if I go, because if I go I can leave behind my Holy Spirit.' And he breathed on the disciples, and he said 'receive my Spirit'. Now the Holy Spirit isn't coming and going like in the Old Testament times; neither is it like in Matthew 10 when it came on the disciples as they went on assignment – now it's a permanent filling. As Jesus ascends to heaven he leaves behind the Holy Spirit, so that all over the world the Spirit's moving through anointed people who go out in the power of the Holy Spirit.

And it's for us, 2,000 years later, because there aren't two Holy Spirits! There isn't a watered-down 'English' kind of Holy Spirit that's a bit wet and wimpy, it's the same Holy Spirit that he poured out on those first disciples. We're meant to move in the fullness and go out in the power of the Holy Spirit. Don't you want more of it? Don't we need to get filled afresh and then step out in faith, speak boldly as we preach the gospel? We're selling people short if we don't.

A high calling

Maybe we all need to do a little health check here. How are you doing in terms of preaching good news to the poor? How often do the words of life come out of your mouth? How often do you preach Jesus to your friends and neighbours and relevantly come alongside them? Not just on a stage because you get paid for it, or it's just what you do because you're in a Message band, but how much is that the heartbeat of your life? Your answer to that question is sure evidence of just how filled you are.

How much do you love the poor? How much do you bind up the broken-hearted? How often do you get involved in setting captives free? I think sure evidence of whether you're filled with the Spirit is how well you can answer that question; how much is that your heart? Do you long to see the broken set free, the prisoners blessed, the most marginalised, hurting members of society healed? If that's you, there's good evidence you're filled.

How about this for a challenge: how often do you lay your hands on the sick with faith and expectancy? How often do you step out in faith to see blind eyes open and as you go, see the dead raised? Jesus said, 'As you go, preach the good news of the kingdom, raise the dead, bind up the broken-hearted, cleanse the lepers'. You can only do that because Jesus said 'Receive my Spirit as the Father sent me, I'm sending you'. As the Father sent Jesus out of the desert three-and-a-half years previously, he's sending you now.

We need to wake up to just how high our calling is. It may not be that we're the guy to preach good news to the poor, to millions like Reinhard Bonnke – but let's do it to one or two and see what happens. Maybe we're not the next Mother Teresa who's going to set up massive work in the slums of Calcutta, so we're just going to find some hurting people who leave nearby and bless them. Maybe we're not going to have the next power evangelism ministry or write the books but we're just going to lay our hands on some sick people and see what happens. How about it? How about being people like that?

REFLECTION

1. Search online for a list of prophecies that Jesus fulfilled from the Old Testament and marvel at the ways God arranged history to shine a spotlight on the Messiah.

2. At times we too can be 'blinded by brokenness and fear'. Pray that Jesus will open your eyes to things you are blind to today.

3. Do you dare follow Andy's instructions to do a heart health check and examine your response to the poor?

PRAYER

Lord, help us to wake up to the high calling you place on our lives – to love the poor with all we have. Give us boldness to step out with expectant faith that you'll move as we pray in your powerful name.

Amen

'...a real key for people
sticking with their faith is
feeling part of a community
and finding real friends'

TONY GRAINGE

Shortly after becoming a Christian in 2002 I went travelling to Australia for a year. One Friday I found myself in Hillsong Church in Sydney visiting their youth club. I was so impressed by it, I was inspired to start something in Easterside where I lived that would have young people loving Jesus and being completely unashamed of him. So I started volunteering as a youth worker for the church in 2003 before being employed by the church in 2007 and going full-time for Eden in 2011.

Growing up on Easterside there were stolen cars driving around the estate, a high rate of burglaries, boarded-up houses and lots of anti-social behaviour from teenagers. Today all these crimes have dramatically reduced. Last year a gang of teenagers smashed a window on the estate and there was uproar with all the residents complaining and making a big deal of it. To me, it showed how far forward Easterside has moved when such a big deal is made over a broken window, when that kind of activity was common a few years ago.

We have a team of eight people on Easterside and of that eight, four became Christians though the work we have done. That has always been our vision – to create disciples who make disciples. We've had three people who've won Urban Hero Awards for volunteering and turning

their lives around. (We would have had four winners, except that one lad, Dean, wouldn't accept it as he thought it would be embarrassing making a video!) We also have ten associate members on the team who don't live on the estate but volunteer their time at least once a week – and five of them became Christians though our work too.

We make an effort to meet people where they are at – through detached work, at the local gym, running football teams and just eating food together. Then we invite them to something where they can hear the gospel and or experience the Holy Spirit like Alpha courses, guest services or baptisms. Many young people have made commitments through these things. What has been massive for our older lads like Andy and Luay is doing a year out with the church. Four of them have completed what we call the Daniel Challenge which has been great for their faith, confidence and knowledge. It has helped them become very valuable members of our team too.

We've learned over the years a real key for people sticking with their faith is feeling part of a community and finding real friends. So we run groups to grow in relationship with each other, learn more about our faith and to pray for each other. My wife Steph and I run a house group with adults over 30, our friends Ben and Jess run one for 20-30s and we have Andy, Luay and Aleks whose house

(Clockwise from top left): Luay; Andy; a midweek service in
Easterside; Andy, Tony and Luay

has become a great meeting place for people in their early 20s.

Off the back of Eden we recently started a Wednesday night midweek service. We started it for two reasons: people don't believe in God because they have never encountered him, and that even after people have they often don't stick with church because they don't feel part of it. So we set the night up based around good quality food and conversation, worship, testimonies to raise faith, a short message and opportunities to be prayed for at the end. We've been running for three months now and the response from people has been superb. Each week people have been meeting with God in a variety of ways and each week people have been making commitments to follow him. We've had some great comments from people who come. All these are from people who aren't Christians yet: 'I was looking forward to helping out with something after retirement, and this is it', 'I love being part of something that's growing and helps so many people', 'I look forward to Wednesdays more than a night out.'

I struggle with Eden taking credit for what has happened in Easterside, as there have been a few key organisations on the estate who have worked really well together. The local kids' club, St Agnes Church, councillors, gym and loads of others have made Easterside a great place to live. What we can take credit for is the individuals' lives who've been touched and transformed through a relationship with Jesus and through the help and support of the Eden team and the church.

ANDY WALKER

In 2011 a supernatural encounter with Jesus changed my life completely. I walked into a church in Stockton-on-Tees as a man who was angry and carrying a lot of pain from a violent past and walked out of that same church as a man who was free. God did for me in two minutes what therapy and counselling couldn't do in two years – he gave me the strength to forgive my Dad and myself, and replaced my anger and chaos with peace and joy.

My Dad had some health problems growing up which caused lots of stress at home. I no longer blame him for what happened, thanks to God who has completely restored our relationship, and I am proud to say I love my Dad very much, but it wasn't always like that. At the time I blamed myself a lot for what was going on at home, always thinking that if I had been braver, stronger or faster I could have prevented it. So I started lashing out, doing drugs, drinking and fighting. That's what I was like that night in the church in Stockton.

I remember clearly how it happened. Tony Grainge was praying for me and he said that I needed to forgive my Dad. I told him I couldn't, so Tony asked me to ask God to help me. I remember a massive weight being lifted from my shoulders when I did this and an overwhelming sense of peace came upon me. Words cannot really describe how I felt – I felt like skipping home, I felt at peace, I felt loved.

God is still doing massive things in my life, five years on. One of the biggest miracles is that God in his great wisdom and power got this young lad forged in the heart of

Boro's council estates into university! I am studying to be a social worker so I can help children who have come from similar backgrounds as me, and also to help the men responsible for violence to let them know they are loved too, and that God forgives them.

LUAY HIZAN

I experienced a troubled, unstable childhood as a kid. My parents split up when I was young and I lost contact with my father. Throughout my early years we seemed to be moving from place to place, due to a new relationship my mother was involved in for a long while. This man was intimidating, addicted to drugs and emotionally abusive towards me and my mother and for various reasons we had to keep moving.

My life all through school was spent in environments I shouldn't have being around, hearing conversations I shouldn't have heard and seeing things I shouldn't have seen. School was an escape, but only just – I was bullied and I was a bully towards others. I had no direction and no aspirations which gained me nothing but no grades and no friends once it was all over. Honestly, I hated my life, and I locked myself away from the world. I developed anxiety and depression which completely changed who I was, and always for the worse.

Until – and this is where my story gets brighter – I met a Christian called Andy Walker at college. He invited me to a meal around a friend's house and I met Tony Grainge, who was talking about the Holy Spirit in such a simple way that made sense.

At the end of the meal he invited the Holy Spirit to make his presence known and impact us. And he did that night. I was eager to know more and went along to a summer camp with the church. There I was prayed for and I experienced an overwhelming fire in my belly and felt like the only one in the room. I burst out in joy and emotion, I was happy and I was crying at the same time. This sparked the flame that is still burning today. Five years on, and I have been a missionary in Eastern Europe, am back in education (doing a degree in mental health nursing) and I'm telling people about Jesus as part of the Eden Network. Ultimately, I am a changed person. I truly am born again. God is so good!

I'm 'Boro born and bred' – I have lived pretty much all around Middlesbrough all my life, so I know that what is happening now, particularly in Easterside where we have the Eden team, is unprecedented. This estate is changing more rapidly than it ever has, and people from all around the estate and outside it are hearing about the reasons why.

GOD WILL HAVE A PEOPLE

CHAPTER ELEVEN

ISAIAH 65:1, 17-19

'I revealed myself to those who did not ask for me;

    I was found by those who did not seek me.

To a nation that did not call on my name,

    I said, "Here am I, here am I."'

'See, I will create

    new heavens and a new earth.

The former things will not be remembered,

    nor will they come to mind.

But be glad and rejoice for ever

    in what I will create,

for I will create Jerusalem to be a delight

    and its people a joy.

I will rejoice over Jerusalem

    and take delight in my people;

the sound of weeping and of crying

    will be heard in it no more.'

Isaiah 65:1, 17-19

"

It's amazing that we have the right to say 'no' to God. But we do

I t really is true to say that 'All over the world the Spirit is moving.' I recently had the privilege of being invited to speak at the Exponential Conference in Orlando with 5,000 or so church planters from all around the world. It was so encouraging to hear what God is doing all around the world – in China, in Africa, India... there are fires of revival burning all over the world!

Do you realise that the number of Christians on Planet Earth has trebled in the last hundred years? In fact, there's never been a time in history when people were becoming Christians faster. A hundred years ago, over two-thirds of the world's Christians lived in Europe, but in the last hundred years there's been an incredible explosion in all these places that were previously so dark.

I am convinced that Jesus is coming soon. I'm not saying he's coming tomorrow (though he might!) but every day I want to be on tiptoes of expectation. I want to be saying, 'God, I can see what you're doing on the Earth and I want to be part of it, so when I see you face to face I get that 'Well done, good and faithful servant.' I want to be part of the action wherever it's happening.

Rejecting his advances

And so we've got up to Isaiah 65. We're coming to the end of the book, and here I think Isaiah is summing up. The whole book is based on this: God will have a people and God's purposes will prevail. Isaiah is a book of salvation and judgement, and you can't have one without the other. A lot of the church, I think, nowadays wants the salvation story without the judgement story. But there's no real salvation unless you're being saved *from* something. We're being saved from judgement because of what Christ did. God reaches out to a people, determined to have a people who will share his glory and experience the blessing of being, as the song goes, 'no longer a slave to fear but a child of God'.

Isaiah in the temple says, 'Here I am, send me', but Isaiah could only say 'Here I am, send me' because God first said, 'Here I am, seek me'. Listen to the first three verses of Isaiah chapter 65 and tell me this is not beautiful...

'I revealed myself to those who did not ask for me;

I was found by those who did not seek me.

To a nation that did not call on my name,

I said, "Here am I, here am I."' (Isaiah 65:1)

God will have a people. He will populate heaven. He will have a family. He will have friends who share in his glory and work alongside him – what a massive privilege! But despite all he's done to reach out to us – ultimately, of course, sending his own son to die for us – if we choose to live for ourselves and reject his advances and pursue injustice and unrighteousness instead, after so long, God will accept our decision. It's tragic. But that's what love is like.

What if I pursue my wife Michele, and she rejects my advances? If she goes off with loads of other blokes, smashes up my house, and wastes all our resources? After so long I'd have to say 'Despite my great love for you, Michele, we ain't got a relationship here, have we?' Now that is not my story, praise the Lord, but the comparison stands. After so long of God pursuing us saying 'Here I am, here I am.... Look, here I am, even willing to die for you!' If after so long all we do is choose unrighteousness and build our own kingdoms, well ultimately God is going to underline it. He's going to leave us to it.

So here in Isaiah 65 we hear those terrible words of just what that looks like. In verses 13 and 14 the Sovereign Lord says, 'My servants will eat, but you will go hungry. My servants will drink; you will go thirsty. My servants will rejoice but you will be put to shame. My servants will sing out of the joy of their hearts but you will cry out from anguish and wail in brokenness of spirit.' What a terrible picture of someone who's chosen to go their own way, build their own kingdom, live their own life, say 'No, God'. What a stupid thing to do! It's amazing that we have the right to say 'no' to God. But we do.

White elephant

Before the Exponential Conference in Orlando, Michele and I had a few days in the Bahamas-poor us! Down the road from where we were staying is a hotel complex called the Bahama Hotel. It was meant to be a game-changer for the Bahamas, destined to transform the country's economy. It was going to put their GDP up by 12%. It's a three-and-a-half billion-dollar development, with 2300 bedrooms, a luxury casino, a massive golf course designed by Jack Nicklaus. I think I'm right in saying it's the single largest development in the world at the moment.

And yet the project has gone bankrupt at 97% complete. So instead of transforming the economy for good, it's transformed the economy for ill. There's even a threat of it bringing down the entire Bahamian economy, because businesses associated with it are going bust all over the place. It's got everything there, it's even got the glass in the windows. The golf course is finished but no-one is playing. Nothing's happening as the lawyers fight over it. While we were there, people were saying, 'We don't think it's ever going to open'. Thousands of people over so many years have worked so hard to build a massive white elephant.

To me, it feels like a little picture of what God's talking about here in Isaiah 65: we can put all our efforts and resources into building a life that looks amazing but that ultimately is useless and empty and bankrupt. It's possible to have it all, but still be empty because we haven't turned to the Saviour. That's the picture Isaiah paints: 'Come on people, look at all I've got for you. Look at all you can enjoy, look at all the blessings of walking with God... but you choose to go your own way, you choose to pursue your own agenda. So all I can do is underline that and say we can't have a relationship because you don't want a relationship.'

A better vision

But that's not for us. For us it's this: pictured in verse 17-19: 'See, I will create new heavens and a new earth. The former things will not be remembered, nor will they come to mind. But be glad and rejoice for ever in what I will create, for I will create Jerusalem to be a delight and its people a joy. I will rejoice over Jerusalem and take delight in my people; the sound of weeping and of crying will be heard in it no more.'

Do you like the sound of it? That's your destiny if you know Jesus. Because you've been forgiven, because you've been accepted. Because you're walking with him.

And when you read on, you find that there's more. There is a place of no chemotherapy, no premature deaths, no stillbirths. Anybody reading this sick? Anybody sad? Anybody stressed? Anybody skint? Here on earth, don't be surprised about that: 'Do not be surprised at the fiery ordeal that has come on you to test you, as though something strange were happening to you' (1 Peter 4:12). No, this side of heaven there are painful trials that we face.

But we've got a vision that keeps us going – a vision of a new heaven and a new earth when it's all going to be made right. It's a place we're going. Of course we want God to break in at any moment and deliver us from life's difficulties, here and now and indeed he can. But as we journey, the vision of heaven keeps us going. You begin to see why the slave songs are so profound – these people who are treated so terribly with such appalling injustice, yet their songs were 'Soon and very soon, I'm going be with the King...', their songs were songs of glory. They had a vision and they know that this can't be all there is. This can't be heaven here; there is going to be a new heaven and a new earth.

Sometimes I feel like we have our eggs in the wrong basket. We expect all the blessings to be here, when actually more than 99.9% of the blessings are going to be there. They're still to come, in this new Heaven and this new Earth. I think sometimes we picture heaven like a kind of upgrade of life as we know it now. But actually no, no, no, heaven is not an upgrade – it's a totally new order of things. It's not just everything turned around; it's everything turned the right way up.

The reality is, we'll all be there in a hundred years' time, because we know Jesus and we've decided to say yes. We've decided to say 'Here I am, send me' in response to him saying 'Here I am, seek me'.

REFLECTION

1. Do you sometimes feel like amid all the 'doom and gloom' news of church decline in the UK and Europe we're missing something? We are! Spend a few moments reading faith-building stories of revival around the world online.

2. Where might God be trying to make himself known in new ways in your life at the moment?

3. Read the whole of Isaiah 65 and spend a little time thinking about what the 'new heavens and new earth' will be like.

PRAYER

Thank you Jesus, that you are reaching into the hardest, most broken lives and saying 'Here I am, here I am'. Lord, we pray for many more glorious testimonies to come. And whatever the cost, we say it's worth it, Lord. All the trials, all the difficulties, all the challenges, to see your kingdom come, and see lives put back together for you.

Amen

'...as you walk humbly with an Almighty God, the Almighty happens'

Andy adds: Laura's story is a truly inspirational one to end the book on. It shows what happens when we follow God's heart and serve the poor, and is an amazing example of the 'abundantly more' of God that we see time and time again through Eden.

I first encountered The Message Trust at Message 2000 aged 18. I'd booked in to camp in Heaton Park with my sister and see what happened. We had decided to go because 1) Manchester sounded exciting and we had never been 'up North', 2) we thought hanging out with lots of other young people would always be fun, and, 3) who knew if God really did do things that had been promised in the flyer? With all the prejudice and naïvety of Home Counties girls we fully expected that simply our very presence would change 'the North.' Oh, how I now cringe!

What actually happened that week was that God changed me and set me on a totally different life path.

I discovered a few things that week: that camping is essentially miserable; that my DIY skills in painting a forlorn church hall in Swinton might have not been a blessing to said church; and that God did actually turn up. Day after day, hour after hour God moved and my mind was slowly blown. At the end of the week in an experience I can still only describe as being completely physical, I walked into the MEN Arena and it was as if I walked through a physical wall and God simply said, 'Stay. Stay in Manchester.' From that moment, I did.

The next few months were surreal. I lived with some lovely students from Manchester Uni and lived off money that arrived in envelopes to my door (from where, I have no idea). I returned to the estate I had been on during Message 2000 and more and more people turned to faith and I saw miracles happen. I was so naïve that I literally thought that this is what happens when you play a guitar instead of an organ! I joined Eden Harpurhey that Christmas, living there for three years and having a great time. It was a ball to be living with a team of talented, fun and totally faith-filled young adults. Over the three years, we tried many a tactic to bring the Kingdom to Harpurhey – dance nights, kids' clubs, church services, youth clubs, trips, songs… I look back with a massive smile on my face and giggle at some of the mishaps! In the time I was there God did move – and not always in the ways we were loudly demanding of him. Most of all, God worked in me. I started to see that life is not led in straight lines, that opportunity is not equal, that poverty is pervasive, that darkness really does prevail in our inner cities, and yet hope and light and grace can break through and set people free.

After three years, I moved from Harpurhey. My wedding day was a mix of emotions as I also moved out of an area I had grown to love – never again (so far) have I been to Asda in my PJs! My new husband and I moved to Fitton Hill in Oldham, to start a Eden project and church plant with the Salvation Army. We started the same cycle of Eden again: praying for kingdom, organising the least cool youthie ever delivered under a Message banner (after realising that serving Horlicks rather than

sweets improved behaviour). Meanwhile, I continued with my studies at medical school.

Over the next year I became acutely aware that the healthcare my neighbours were experiencing and the medicine I was learning did not correlate. My neighbour had a stroke and didn't get the follow-up she needed with an adult son with learning disabilities. I realised if something were to happen to her, who would look after him? My other neighbour, an alcoholic, was treated with disdain when she fell and broke her wrist. Unable to read the letter sent by the NHS, she did not go to the clinic and never had her wrist fixed, instead becoming permanently disabled. Everywhere I looked, this community was being let down by health services and as a result the health outcomes were shocking.

A lightbulb movement came when I read a piece of academic writing by an amazing man called Julian Tudor Hart called the Inverse Care Law. (Those of you about to switch off, don't.) His research first published in 1970s showed that access to healthcare varies inversely with the needs of the population; in other words, the sickest people, the neediest populations, usually get the least access to healthcare. Tudor Hart was initially ostracised from the medical profession, but his findings have been shown to be true in every country in the world, in every health care service. I know it, because I saw it front of my own eyes, right where I was living. I was bothered by what I saw. I was irritated in my soul.

Over the next few years we campaigned with lots of other agencies in the area for a local health centre. We were joined by the local police, the head teacher, the housing officer, the residents, all asking for a GP practice in Fitton Hill. Eventually the NHS said yes, that they would put in a new practice. My job, I thought, was complete, and yet as I walked out of the office the NHS manager I had argued with for years had one last passing shot: 'You could always bid to run it if you're so passionate.' I flounced round and said, 'I will.'

Hope Citadel Healthcare CIC was formed that day. I was still at medical school, juggling Eden, small children and now googling how to set up a community interest company and to teach myself the basics of HR and cash flow. The vision was simple: to provide the best healthcare possible in areas of deprivation, working creatively, compassionately and never giving up on those in our care. The values were simple: not for profit, driven by passion not by money, endless hope and compassion always telling of grace. A fellow Eden-ite, Dr John Patterson, was hugely supportive and helpful.

Over the last seven years, a small group of us have toiled away to deliver this dream. Some days we get it really right. The CQC, the 'Ofsted for healthcare', rate our Practices as Outstanding, and our 20,000 patients are mostly grateful. Other days it's all still heartbreakingly tough. There is still entrenched poverty, huge human suffering that still makes me cry and stops me in my tracks. There are constant battles for funding, buildings, fairness and justice within the NHS.

This year at our annual doctors' study day I spoke about Matilda, the Roald Dahl character. I love Matilda. She is clever, feisty, she sees problems and situations,

she reads people, she's geeky, creative and persistent in her practice. But she also waits for the miraculous to happen. The journey of Hope Citadel mirrors this tale. When I first joined The Message I was not quite sure how I would fit in – I did ballet dancing instead of break-dancing; I knew more about science than about current TV shows; I had the wrong accent; I didn't know what a 'ginnel' was. On paper I was one of the least likely people to do anything meaningful in an area of deprivation. I was essentially a scared geek. And like Matilda, as my heart has changed – I've seen my miraculous happen.

Nine years ago I sat alone at a 24/7 prayer meeting. Bored and unable to pray, I started drawing. I drew a building that was a health centre called Hope in the middle of Fitton Hill with stained-glass windows at the front. I thought nothing of the picture. Just five years later I walked into the nearly-finished health centre. I had not paid much attention to the building going up as I was working lots of shifts as a junior doctor and it was all handled by the NHS architects and, being very grateful for a permanent building at all, I didn't really care what it looked like. As I walked from the back corridor into the waiting room for the first time, I was met by a double-height space, complete with stained-glass windows. It was just as I had drawn it all those years before.

Seventeen years later on, I'm so glad I booked into Message 2000. So follow the agitation of your heart, be quietly stubbornly determined to use all your skills to bring justice, mercy and kingdom… and as you walk humbly with an Almighty God, the Almighty happens.

THE
FAVOUR OF
GOD

CHAPTER TWELVE

ISAIAH 66:2-3

'These are the ones I look on with favour:

    those who are humble and contrite in spirit,

    and who tremble at my word.

But whoever sacrifices a bull

    is like one who kills a person,

and whoever offers a lamb

    is like one who breaks a dog's neck;

whoever makes a grain offering

    is like one who presents pig's blood,

and whoever burns memorial incense

    is like one who worships an idol.

They have chosen their own ways,

    and they delight in their abominations;

so I also will choose harsh treatment for them

    and will bring on them what they dread.'

Isaiah 66:2-3

"

Whatever you do, find your place in the mission of God

In his final chapter, Isaiah describes two kinds of people: 'Those are the ones I look on with favour, those who are humble and contrite in spirit, and who tremble at my word' (v.2) and those who 'have chosen their own ways, and they delight in their abominations; so I also will choose harsh treatment for them and will bring on them what they dread' (vv.3-4). I know which I want to be – how about you?

Do you want to be that person on whom the favour of God rests, someone who knows the smile of God on their life? Someone who remains confident that, through all the challenges and difficulties of life, they are at the centre of God's will, and that his will in prevailing their life? Or do you want to be the kind of person who experiences harsh treatment, and on whom the Lord brings what they dread?

I think in lots of ways – even as God's people – we get to choose. Once you've given your life to Christ, our eternal destination is secure. We're going to be in heaven because it's not about what we do, it's about what he did. On that day of true surrender, and true repentance, and true commitment to Christ, that much is decided. But how much we then choose to walk in the favour of God, and the extent to which we actually experience his hand on our life is down to us, every day. We've got our salvation, yes. But what about our sanctification?

Good choices

In closing my book, I want to say a few things which I think sum up Isaiah's 66 amazing chapters. The first thing is: don't be stupid. Make good choices – make godly choices – and it will go not just well with you, but well with the nation. I believe the future of a nation is not decided by its parliament; it's decided by the church of Jesus Christ, by his people. How we behave and what we do with our lives affects the future of this nation. We at The Message are not going to change culture not simply by doing loads of massive youth gigs or launching record number of Edens, but by being a people who are set apart for Jesus – a people who are walking in repentance. Don't allow unconfessed and cherished sin into your relationship with God – it's just not worth it. Why would you want to be any other place than holy, pure and righteous in your walk and ascending the hill of the Lord, as Isaiah paints here?

It's a sad thing to meet backslidden Christians, when the fire's gone out of their eyes. I recently heard about an awesome evangelist who fell out of ministry after a moral failure. He now gets paid forty thousand dollars a pop for doing high-level business presentations for a large American firm. Maybe in the world's eyes this man still looks like a success – but how tragic that he's no longer winning souls for Jesus and is now lecturing to businessmen on how to get richer still! If the calling of your life is as an evangelist, a soul winner, a breakthrough person, but then you lower your standards because sin gets in, that's what will happen. I don't want that to be the mark on my life – do you? I want to go all the way.

Thankfully there's always a way back with Jesus. Two years ago on Father's Day, I was preaching in Bradford, and I got chatting to a guy in the car park afterwards. It was his first time in church for eight years, because he'd got really bitter and fallen out with God. He was in really a bad place – his marriage was in a mess, and he was dangerously overweight – but in the car park that Father's Day I had the privilege of leading him back to Jesus. Imagine my surprise and delight when, fast forward two years, I'm back in Bradford to speak again at the same church, and who should show up but the same guy! I had to do a double-take, because he's lost more than twent stone, he's on fire for Christ, his marriage is really strong, he's leading a life group and he's an evangelist in the church!

What a picture of one person living with the Lord's favour, over and against the one who's chosen their own ways.

Listen up!

I also think Isaiah reminds us to get in a place where we can hear the Lord who speaks. For some of us, honestly, our spiritual disciplines are a joke. You're not going to hear the Lord unless you're disciplined in your Bible study, and you're disciplined in your prayer life. The Lord wants to speak, the Lord loves to speak. Yes, the Lord is constantly saying 'here I am, seek me' and 'See, I'm doing a new thing. Do you not perceive it?' – that's his part. Our part is perceiving what the Lord is saying, and getting on with doing what he says.

I heard a really beautiful story from a lady called Emma recently. She said she was in a queue in a shoe shop in Scotland, when she felt the Lord say, 'You need to speak to that girl behind the counter – I've got a word for her.'

Understandably, she was a bit reluctant with it being a shoe shop. But soon, the queue faded away so it was just her and the girl, so Emma plucked up the courage to say, 'I think the Lord wants to say this to you'. She didn't even know what was going to come out of her mouth, but she said, 'You're going to be a great mother'. That's what came out of her mouth, 'You're going to be a great mother.' Suddenly the girl started crying, and said: 'That's amazing, because I've just found out I'm pregnant and I've booked the abortion in. But I've prayed, "Oh God, I feel bad about it. Even though I haven't prayed for years, please help me in this situation," and you came into the shop and said, "You're going to be a great mother."' So Emma then watched as the girl went to the phone and cancelled the abortion. Amazing. How amazing that we can hear Jesus, that God's heart can be poured out through us, that we can see lives change and families restored and babies saved and salvation come, as we just walk in obedience to his voice?

You see, he didn't just speak in the past but speaks to his people now. And not just every day, but every moment, the Lord wants to be in conversation with us.

I want to be open and expectant of the voice of the living God speaking to me. I love the fact that Isaiah finishes his book with this great charge to mission. Verse 19: 'I will set a sign among them, and I will send some of those who survive to the nations – to Tarshish, to the Libyans and Lydians, to Tubal and Greece, and to the distant islands that have not heard of my fame or seen my glory. They will proclaim my glory among the nations.' Can you hear God's heart for mission there? It's a theme of the whole book. God speaks in all kinds of different ways just to stir his people to mission.

And that's the message I want to end this book on: whatever you do, find your place in the mission of God. We've all got a part to play. We're all on a mission because God wants be known among the nations. Don't write yourself off because you think of yourself as a 'background person'. We need faithful people serving behind the scenes as well as the ones up the front. But we all need to be thinking, 'I'm going to reach people for Jesus. I'm going to be praying for my family. I'm going to be stepping out in faith myself.' God gets great glory through ordinary people like us, setting our lives apart to his purpose, finding our place in his mission, and seeing transformation come in Jesus' name as a result and honestly there is no more exciting and worthwhile life than that.

REFLECTION

1. 'You're not going to hear the Lord unless you're disciplined in your Bible study, and you're disciplined in your prayer life.' Who could you ask to help you with hearing the Lord more clearly at this point in your life?

2. It's essential that we are walking in repentance. Perhaps as you were reading, the Holy Spirit was identifying something in your life. If so, sort it out with the Lord now.

3. As we close this book, please pray for the Message staff and volunteer team, especially anyone you know personally: that they would stay on fire for God and passionate for the lost.

PRAYER

Father, thank you for calling me into a living relationship with you through your Son. Thank you for anointing me and equipping me for your mission in the world. Help me to remain 'humble and contrite in spirit' and obedient to your Word, and to know your favour today and for the rest of my life.

Amen

NOTES

The Message Trust

The Message Trust is a worldwide movement with a passion to share Jesus Christ with the hardest-to-reach young people. Through a dynamic combination of creative mission, community transformation and Christ-centred enterprise, we witness to the transforming power of the gospel of Jesus in words and actions.

The mark of a life changed by Jesus is the desire to see others changed too. Time and time again, we see young people going from being the problem to the solution thanks to our work. Many members of our mission teams were once drug abusers, dealers or violent criminals themselves.

We celebrate our stories in print through Flow magazine and in books like this one; online at **www.message.org.uk** and through regular podcasts; and at special events such as our annual Urban Hero Awards in Manchester.

The story doesn't end here...

Want to see more of what you've been reading about?
Want to look back and say, 'I was a part of that'?
Let's make some history together.

COME

Join our Message Academy and discover your part in God's mission.
Ten months of intense training and frontline mission placements in the dynamic,
faith-filled atmosphere of The Message in Manchester.

message.org.uk/academy

GO

Called to urban neighbourhoods? Eden needs you.
Join the UK's gutsiest mission movement and bring the hope of the gospel
to forgotten communities. Join an existing team or lead a new one.

joineden.org

GIVE

Help take our work to the next level by standing with us financially.
We're looking for 1,000 new supporters to give **£25 per month**.
Could you help in this way or send a one-off gift?

message.org.uk/donate

PRAY

Prayer is the fuel to all we do.
Sign up to receive our bi-monthly Prayer Calendar.

message.org.uk/pray

For more information on all the above, you can also call 0161 946 2300